TRAUMA IS A TEAM SPORT

How to Turn Tragedy into Goal-Crushing Motivation

Tyson Dever authored with Sarah Paulk

The events retold in this book have been written based on personal recollection, eyewitness accounts, news reports and medical records. They have been relayed to the best of my knowledge. To protect privacy, some identities may have been changed.

ISBN-13: 978-1-9840-0019-4

To Mom and Dad, Justin and Dustin, for your
unconditional love and support.

CONTENTS

ACKNOWLEDGMENTS

The authors thank the people on the front lines of this tragedy, whose honesty and bravery helped bring this book to life: Phillip, Daryl, Ryan, Kevin, Stef and J.R., whose courage, skill and selfless actions saved a life; Amber and her family, who valiantly walked an incredibly difficult road; and Martha and Henry Dever, heroically supportive parents, without whom this story would have had a much different ending.

To the friends and family who stood on the sidelines cheering us on, there are not enough ways to express our gratitude. To Brock Paulk, for never allowing the second guesses to take over, to Brooks and Audrey, who continue to patiently share Mom with words, and to Mary Wilhite who planted the dream, it is because of your encouragement that these pages are full.

Thank you to Trey Jackson for your imaginative cover art, to Deana Nall for improving us with your editing prowess and to Melanie Larson for pointing us in the right direction.

And most of all, to the countless students, teachers, colleagues, leaders, clients and friends who requested this book into reality: thank you for believing in us. May it change you as it has changed us. Blessings.

INTRODUCTION

I t didn't begin this way for me, of course. The life I was born into and the one I live in now are at once excruciatingly different and reassuringly similar. That's the odd thing about drastic, body-altering changes. When a disability is all you've ever known, I would imagine it's a little easier to embrace as part of who you are. When it crashes into your already established identity, as it did to me, it can feel like a swift injustice, ripping the breath right out of your lungs.

No one expects the worst will happen, but it can and some would say that it did to me. It's an insult that it dared to happen in the prime of my life, at the age of 22 and only months before I reached the pinnacle of everything I had invested in and worked toward: my education, my career, my marriage. As you'll discover, not all of those investments worked out the way I had imagined. Some came to life in ways I hadn't dreamed, while others were choked out by the weeds of despair and grief. When the worst happens, nothing remains untouched.

The aftershocks of a catastrophe of this magnitude never really go away. The dust settles and life goes on, but the repercussions remain. That's why I've dedicated myself to telling and retelling how I overcame the most difficult and painful moments of my life to friends as well as perfect strangers. I've had firsthand experience watching others be taken down unnecessarily by their own worst moments. I've seen people give up and ruin their lives because the consequences of their own misfortunes were too great. I found myself in that same place and recognized that I, too, was at a crossroad, staring down the painful footpaths of both freedom and death. It is one of my greatest blessings that I discovered how to muster the strength and courage to choose a future built on hope, but I do not look down on those who could not. For me, it feels not just selfish, but almost heartless to keep that formula for survival to myself and secret.

To that end, I have spent the past decade crisscrossing the country, speaking to schools, student councils, corporate teams and organizations, sharing the good moments along with the bad, to provide others with the tools I found that helped me reassemble my life when it seemed everything had fallen apart. I've seen how these action steps and resources can positively affect the lives of others, regardless of age or circumstance, and I know it can speak into your life as well. It continues to surprise and delight me how my one lifetime of challenges has cast new light on difficult situations, throbbing heartaches and tough choices for thousands of people. I hope it will do the same for you.

The pages ahead will be filled with vulnerable details about the emotions and intricacies of living through tragedy. You'll be privy to moments of heartbreak and triumph that feel too intimate to share at a dinner party but have been let loose in ink in the following chapters. In those moments, you may feel as though you're standing behind a cracked door, eavesdropping on both the best and worst my life has had to offer. As you leaf through those pages, you may be tempted to pull away out of respect, but I want to invite you instead to lean in. Press your ear against the door and take in everything you can, allowing yourself to absorb what I gained from having so much stripped away.

I have laid my story bare not because I'm especially generous or find it easy to be transparent. To the contrary, I'd probably fit squarely into whatever stereotype you have acquired of a thirty-something male born and raised in Texas. I drive a truck, own a boat, more than a few of my walls are covered in taxidermy animals and my southern drawl probably sounds exactly the way you're imagining.

No, I tell my story because it isn't just about me. It's about you, too.

PART ONE: WRECKAGE

March 11, 2005: The remains.

1 ONE LEFT TURN

It should have been raining.

When I think back to how bright the sun was that morning and how it radiated warmth on my skin, it's difficult to understand how the day turned out the way it did. In the movies, there is always some tease to foreshadow how the bottom will soon fall out for the main character. Scary music will slowly rise in the background or lightning will burst in cackling strikes across dark and distant clouds. But on March 11, 2005, the skies didn't tip their hand. If my world was about to fall apart, nothing in creation was willing to spill the secret.

There isn't much about the morning I remember. Not because my memory is blank, although there are hours missing from my mental record, but because it was just a typical morning. As far as I knew, it wasn't a milestone day. It was just a typical Friday and there wasn't anything worthy of committing to memory.

Like every morning before it, I left my car keys on the nightstand and ran to the gym for cardio before lifting weights and running the same route back home. I don't remember shaking off the night's sleep. I don't remember digging wrinkled athletic shorts out of the laundry pile in the corner of my apartment. And, hauntingly, I don't remember the sensation of my feet pounding against cracked sidewalks and crushing pebbles into gravel drives along my route. The morning's events only remain part of my memory bank because of the countless other mornings it matched.

I can see the path in my mind's eye clearly. The stairs I would take, bounding down two at a time, from my apartment landing to the patchy lawn at the bottom of the rusted railing. I can hear the traffic pattern on repeat, as though the garbage truck rattling past our parking lot dumpster was what really woke the sun. And I can feel the perfect morning air that makes San Marcos, Texas, in March brag worthy. Texas summers scorched, but its springtime, especially spring mornings, were that Goldilocks "just right" that took the edge off the rest of the day. My senses can reproduce that day in March. I can see the mirror image reflection of it through the lens of days before it. What I can't do is remember that day–March 11.

I see still pictures of that morning in my mind like Polaroids snapping every few minutes that help me string the events together. It was Friday, the last day in a week of midterms and the final hours before a week-long break from school. The morning exams would fill the parking lot, drawing even habitual skippers to class. Even though Texas State University's lenient absence policy made class optional for some, midterms were the exception. It was an exaggerated joke that some students would have to introduce themselves to the professors before grabbing an exam and taking their seat, as it might be their first time to have met. But by afternoon, the parking lot would slowly empty as students poured out of their obligatory classes and into cars packed high with either suitcases bound for vacation or piles of dirty clothes bound for their parents' laundry rooms.

Midterms made Texas State feel like a ghost town and I planned to be one of the reasons it was vacant. Campus would be quiet but the surrounding towns would inevitably explode with activity. Spending spring break in Central Texas, where the college party scene has staked a claim in state lore for wild rages fueled by Shiner Bock and Lone Star Beer, is a rite of passage for thousands of college students in Texas every year. Then, as it does now, Texas State earned its reputation for partying. Thirty minutes away, the University of Texas at Austin, with its 6th Street bar crawls, makes Texas State look more like a seminary or divinity school. During spring break, those campuses, along with other nearby schools, are beckoned by the San Marcos River. Together, their campuses' worth of barely-legal co-eds meet and mingle to float down an intoxicated river of beer bongs and Jell-O shots, turning Central Texas in March into a scene that rivals *Animal House*. Many of the stories seem wildly blown out of proportion, and many are. But working as a bartender for more than half my time living there, I can say with certainty that many of those stories have at least a measure of credibility to them.

Bar crawls were nowhere on my radar that first day of spring break. If it's possible for a college-aged male to get sick of tequila, I was there. Forty to 50 hours of my week were spent standing behind a bar at the Texican Café in Austin pouring, mixing and wiping up spills from cocktails, draft beer and shots of "the hard stuff," as one of my regulars used to say. Most nights found me shifting my weight from one damp non-slip shoe to the other, waiting for last call and cleaning out crusted beer tap nozzles. I've read that the sense of smell has the power to bring back memories more vividly than sight or hearing possibly can. For me, the pungent smell of hardened yeast will forever be hardwired into my scent memory, filed away under reasons why a college degree is important. It wasn't a bad job, but it owned me. The last thing I wanted to do was loan it more time than I owed.

Spring break 2005 was a week that had been planned and anticipated for months. No work, no class, not even the gym. I spent the night before it alternating between studying for midterm exams and procrastination packing. I couldn't help but feel a buzz, bolstered by caffeine and the idea that the next day would find me beach-ward bound. Most days were spent walking between classes or standing behind a bar, but the knowledge that the Gulf of Mexico was only a few hours of road time away somehow softened the blow of that monotony. Even if I worked out, showered and made it on time to class, I could jump in my car and be toes in the sand by lunch. The next day, my toes actually would be.

Bartending six days a week put a damper on most travel plans, of course. It had been ages since I had even a weekend to myself and this spring break promised a full seven days. But there was more to this getaway than lounging on the beach and my expectation wasn't really all about time off work. If I allow myself to sift through the relics in my mind that have long since been buried, and excavate the feelings that were turned to ruins years ago, it would be apparent that the week was not about a beach. It was not about sleeping late or the absence of school. It was not about seven straight days without pouring drinks for bad tips. It was about Amber.

ROLLING EMBERS

I don't remember when I decided I wanted to marry her. This, of course, has nothing to do with the mild case of amnesia I incurred and everything to do with the fact that we were not right for each other. At the barely-adult age of 22, passion, comfort, lust and insecurity are powerful, habit-forming pills. Amber was beautiful, smart and raised by a warm Texas family who thought well of me. Our attraction to each other established our relationship, but it was how comfortable and easy the ensuing days, weeks and months felt that kept me coming back for more. We were neither hot nor cold; our relationship simply simmered without much effort.

When the opportunity for an entire week together began to unfold, it became clear that although I would be far from a barstool, I would undoubtedly be vulnerable to intoxication.

Amber's grandparents owned a beach house in Port Aransas, a relaxed Texas hot spot about half an hour east of Corpus Christi, and we had gotten the keys and permission from her family to use it for the week. Port A, as native Texans call it, is not exactly known for pristine white sand beaches. The sand is more mud than dune, with a salty layer of seaweed coating. When you say "seaweed" to people whose only beach experience includes the East or West Coast—or worse, exotic locations like Fiji or Jamaica—it does not conjure up quite the right image. Seaweed that washes up on beaches in the Gulf has its own subcategory, known as sargassum, and it arrives on the shore in smelly clumps that can be miles across, and pile up into towering mounds seemingly overnight. Some years are not as bad as others, to be sure, but when it is a particularly bad year for sargassum, it can be a particularly bad year to rent a beach house. But for us, oceanfront property was still oceanfront, regardless of how beautiful the surrounding sands or how few the palm trees and tropical plants would be in number. And a free week on the beach with the woman I planned to ask to be my wife felt like paradise from where I was standing.

I showered off the sweat of the morning's run, dressed and grabbed the bags I had half-packed, half-stuffed the night before. As I bounded down my apartment steps again, I tried to recount the facts and notes I had memorized. This one final midterm would keep me in town a few hours longer than I wanted. The class, First Aid and Safety, was a mandatory part of my degree plan, but would later seem cruel and ironic given the hours that followed. Tossing my duffel into the back of my silver Corvette, I slammed the hatch and climbed into the driver's seat. My foot instinctively switched between the brake pedal and accelerator as I steered toward campus. Whether my manic studying efforts—read, channel surf, read, do laundry, read, pack my bags—would pay off was unclear.

Our Port A road trip was to kick off in Buda, a small suburb about 25 minutes from campus, where Amber's parents lived. The country roads between San Marcos and Buda are classic Texas. Traffic is minimal and most roads are two-lane. The biggest traffic jams at the time were the result of tractors commuting at 20 miles per hour from one side of rural acreage to the other. Every road could be considered a back road, flanked by pastures and ditches filled with wildflowers or roughly mowed grass. The laid-back drive is fitting for Buda's population, which back then only added up to around 5,000 people. Most of the town commutes to Austin to work, and lives very urbane lifestyles, but their choice to live in Buda was a line in the sand of sorts, and a personal statement for some. Sure, they might drive to the city to make a living, but a house in Buda makes it perfectly clear that the country is where they really want to be. If Austin was an obligation to hype and chaos, Buda was the choice for calm and privacy.

I mentally mapped out the day while walking through the parking lot to class. I imagined each curve in the road that would take me from class to Amber and then the beach. My throat squeezed in on itself, my nerves tensing, as I anticipated the drive through Buda. Even the quaint, faded city limits sign with its four-digit population count, I knew, would make my pulse quicken as I drove past. The butterflies that had been launching about once a week had been multiplying in my stomach to the point that they were now a familiar friend. They took flight as I shoved car keys back into my pocket, on cue with the memory of what I had secretly hidden away in that small town. In the back of a closet in Amber's parents' house, in a small box disguised inside a larger, unassuming shoebox, was a promise and commitment in the form of a ring she didn't yet know existed. We had picked out the setting together months earlier—a gold band that curved around the edges and diamond baguettes that flanked the sides—but the nearly one karat marquise diamond I had purchased and hired a jeweler to place in the center would be a surprise. I had silently practiced the delivery over and over in my mind, how I would ask and how her eyes would shine back at me when she said "yes." The rehearsed scene played across my mind again as I took my seat in class, letting my backpack slide off my shoulders so that it made a thud as it hit the floor. This surprise would be like Christmas and every other holiday rolled into one. This gift, once opened, would send my life accelerating in an entirely different direction–the logical and best direction, I hoped.

Papers fluttered backward through rows of hands until reaching my desk. An analog clock ticked above the professor's desk, echoing against the drywall and cinder block walls. Every extra minute I spent mulling over the questions was another minute shaved off my vacation. I filled in bubbles and scribbled short answers until the exam stared back at me, unfinished but no longer blank. I turned the page to the final question, tapping my heel in rhythm to the seconds ticking by. Finally, a question I remembered studying. I pressed my palm against my forehead and bounced my knee as my mind sorted information until finally recovering the answer in full. I regurgitated my memorized notes onto the answer sheet, flipped the stapled pages shut and pushed up and out of the chair. I took a few easy steps toward the front of the room and added my midterm to the mounting stack of papers on my professor's desk. I caught a glimpse of the clock still ticking overhead: I was right on schedule.

With responsibility behind me, I threw open the outside doors and turned my face up to the sun, thumbs looped into the straps of my mostly empty backpack. The promise of vacation was mood-altering. My car reflected the bright afternoon sun, parked slightly askew in my eagerness. In keeping with my usual road trip rhythm, I dumped out my pockets, stuffing everything into the center console before snapping it shut. My seatbelt clicked into place as I turned the key and my Corvette roared to life. As I pulled out of campus onto Post Road, I stole glances at my fellow spring break emigrants. The attitudes of drivers beside me copied what I was feeling as well. Windows were down and hands hung out the open sides, their fingers catching the warm breeze. With the passing of each car, radios could be heard booming different songs. Pat Green's gravelly voice tumbled out of the car to my left and up and down octaves for a few moments before speeding ahead and out of earshot. Cigarette embers occasionally flicked to the pavement in the lanes in front of me, bouncing and rolling until they turned to ash. The weight of responsibility had been lifted: school was out.

Most cars began merging toward the packed interstate, heading to the river or Austin where parties were already beginning to form. Instead, I peeled off from the crowd onto my favorite back road FM 1626, a road locals knew as 5 Mile Dam Road, and followed the faded yellow dashes stretched out in front of me on the pavement. It was the perfect road trip weather. The day bounced off the hood in blue, producing a distorted copy of the cloudless sky above. I pushed my sunglasses up over the bridge of my nose and leaned back against the headrest. My hands gripped the steering wheel while I took in the wide-open spaces around me, the tall grassy pasture to my right bending over, then standing tall in synch with the light breeze.

Where my memory has failed me on that day, it has made up in spades through the vivid details of that short stretch of highway. The grass was a spring mix of vibrant green and yellow, and wildflowers were shyly beginning to blanket the roadside ditches, only a few yards at a time. A school zone speed limit sign warned that Elm Grove Elementary School would pass by my view on the right. Through my window I could see students scrambling up and down the school's sidewalk, excitedly darting in between teachers and friends as they vied for a chance to climb onto the volunteer firetrucks parked in front of the school. A small pasture stretched beyond the school on both sides and then Amber's parents' neighborhood. Rooftops drew closer as I spotted their quiet street and small country neighborhood. I coasted to a stop, pressed my foot against the brake and flicked on my turn

signal as I waited to turn left onto Hy Road, just yards–
inches, really–away from where Amber and I would begin our
week, and the rest of our lives, together. All that stood
between that was one left turn.

My blinker flashed loudly while I waited.

Click, Clack.

Oncoming traffic headed towards me in the opposite lane.

Click, Clack.

One more car, and then it would be safe to turn.

Click, Clack.

A single cab truck appeared in my rearview mirror, pulling
onto the shoulder to pass me on the right.

Click, Clack.

I watched him intentionally go slightly off road, then
carefully steer around me, returning all four tires to the
pavement.

Click, Clack.

The front left tire first, then the rest, before the roar of
impact overtook my senses.

Had I been near a railroad crossing, I would have assumed
a train had derailed on top of my car. My ears deafened from
the sounds of a wreck I hadn't seen coming, and I felt my
throat tighten through screams. The sun had vanished and in
its place was invasive darkness. Flames licked at my arms,
refusing to turn to ash like the cigarette embers I had seen
only moments ago. Those cinders had room to tumble, and
to talk themselves out of a slow burn. The fire that now
invaded was thirsty. I watched as it leaped from the passenger
side dashboard to the center console, trespassing by inches
with every second that passed. I tried to get my bearings,
twisting and searching for a way to escape, to understand.
Where was the sky? Was I upside down?

Through my questions an eerie realization took hold: My
screams could go unanswered. Could anyone hear the cries I
could barely hear myself? I strained to see the world outside
of my seared and mangled car but was held back by smoke as
the fire around me continued to rage and the heat intensified.

Beautiful weather now betrayed me. Rain. Where was the rain?

My lungs burned as smoke invaded every breath. The steering wheel was no longer the same as it had been just moments ago when I had gripped it, both hands on the wheel and blinker flashing. I fought back against its crushed and oddly shaped remains, pressing and pushing with my hands until my forearms burned from effort, but my body remained inexplicably stuck. I felt my feet cemented to the floorboard and realized it was unlikely that I would be able to free them on my own. A wave of panic washed over me as I once again tried to peer through smoke to find the sun.

The skies held steady, but my storm had just begun.

2 THE BEST LAID PLANS

If I'm honest, I'll admit that the first two decades of my life were easy. Sure, I had the average high school dramas that come with puberty and adolescence, but the disappointments that rocked my sense of well-being weren't high enough on the Richter scale to make my memory's highlight reel. There were a few heated arguments, maybe even a few punches thrown, and a couple of sad, awkward breakups, but the sum of those experiences was positive.

My hometown of Andrews, Texas, was the perfect setting to make mistakes and figure out my strengths and weaknesses while the stakes were low and I was surrounded by a town that, while small, was big on supporting its own. Predictably, Andrews is still little more than a dot on the map–a dusty, quiet pit stop for West Texans headed for vacation in Ruidoso. But living in a town with around only 10,000 other people had its positives. Going to the grocery store or the movie theater or the gas station usually meant running into someone you knew. If you were home sick for a few days from school, it wasn't unusual for someone to bring you your homework and maybe even a meal. The kids I went to church with went to school with me as well, so the highlight of my summer was heading to the mountains of New Mexico for church camp. For a week, we would hike to the tops of mountains for sunset devotionals, eat camp food, and flirt with girls from other youth groups while my parents footed the bill and patted me on the head for doing God's work.

Such close quarters came with its own unique set of cons, though, as well. Knowing most of the town by name or at least association meant just about everyone knew you too, but more importantly, they knew your parents. Andrews, Texas, was about as opposite of hippie living as you could get, but communal parenting was abundant. Even Greg, who owned La Morena, the local hole-in-the-wall Mexican food joint, watched over us and felt empowered to discipline us as he saw fit. Every day during our high school lunch period, my friends and I would skip the cafeteria and instead pile into our trucks and old beat up cars to make the five-minute drive to his small brick building next door to an old warehouse. Calling his place a restaurant would be generous. From the outside looking in, the building appeared to be condemned, but the unsuspecting exterior made Greg's cooking even more famous in our little town, turning La Morena into a hidden gem that only the locals knew about. Greg's Kitchen Sink Burritos, named as such because they included every ingredient he could find but the actual kitchen sink, made up at least a fourth of my nutrition during those years. The appearance inside matched the outside with painted cinder block walls and torn checkered vinyl table cloths. Town legend taught us before we ever stepped foot inside that the entire experience would be almost entirely self-serve. His food was worth it and, as teenage boys, his unconventional standards for running a restaurant made us even more loyal fans. When we walked in, my buddies and I would wave to Greg and then go behind the counter to get our own chips and salsa and drinks. When our order was up, Greg would ring the bell, give us a sideways glance and we knew we had better get up and get it ourselves. After we ate, we would bus our own tables, pick up after ourselves and leave while he watched suspiciously behind a newspaper or book in the corner.

Greg had a specific set of unspoken rules and everyone who ate his food understood the consequences. We had seen what happened when other kids talked back to him or shorted him a few bucks. Greg would not be mocked, and if you ticked him off, you could expect that your next burrito or two would be lined with hot sauce so spicy that you'd have to run outside to throw up. It wasn't a secret. In fact, Greg was proud of how he kept all of us boys in check, bragging about the hot sauce collection he had assembled from all over the world, and how his quest for the hottest one would be never-ending. It was a restaurant management system that wouldn't last long in a big city, but in Andrews, Greg was a strange but endearing part of our hometown charm, like an eccentric uncle at a family reunion. Everyone, kids and adults alike, knew how he operated: Don't make Greg mad, or he'll burn you. This made getting away with anything almost impossible, but didn't stop us from trying.

Andrews High School, like every other high school, could be a minefield of cliques and exclusive clubs that was best navigated in herds. I discovered that being in the middle of a group of likeminded people, even if that crowd couldn't be described as popular, was the best safety net. It became clear that no matter what group I joined, someone was going to make fun of me, someone would exclude me, someone would tell me I wasn't good enough. I remember watching as even the most popular kids were bombarded with the same bullying messages as the kids who felt like they were stuck on the outskirts. The difference? The "cool kids" had the benefit of safety in numbers. Being called out by yourself is a terrifying feeling, but having an insult hurled at you while standing in the protection of your group provides the security and power necessary to own your own identity. For me, there was no question as to who comprised my group. You could find us on the game field, in the weight room and in the gym.

PLAY BALL

As students go, I could probably be described as average. Every year a few of my classmates would end up in after-school tutoring sessions–or worse, summer school–and I would sigh with relief knowing I had dodged that bullet. I studied, of course, but just enough to keep my report card filled with A's and B's. I wasn't smart enough to reach valedictorian status without trying, and I didn't care enough to pursue it the hard way.

Where I slacked off in the classroom, I made up ten-fold on the field and in the weight room. Sports fueled my appetite for competition and the drive to win that the classroom couldn't match. School, at that time, was simply a means to an end. Make good grades, stay eligible, get scouted, play college ball and eventually coach. That was the plan.

At times, West Texas sports seemed like its own religion, with the whole town gathering under stadium spotlights every Friday night to worship. And like the preacher's ability to deliver a sermon is scrutinized over pot roast on Sunday afternoon, so too the coach's ability to pull out a win would surely be analyzed the following day over lukewarm cups of coffee poured into chipped coffee mugs at the local town diner. When the team was on a winning streak, coaches would get pats on the back and free lunches around town. When the losses outnumbered the wins, coaches couldn't walk down the cereal aisle without having their shopping carts crashed into by strangers who wanted to give advice on everything from calling plays to superstitions that could make all the difference.

Sports are serious business in Texas and football is king. Movies and TV shows love to embellish what high school football in Texas is all about, but admittedly they're not too far off base. High school sports in small town Texas are followed by just about everyone, regardless of whether you are related to anyone on the team. Local restaurants displayed group photos of the varsity teams in their front windows and installed messages on their marquees that read "Go Mustangs!" year-round. Caravans of pickup trucks and family sedans would make the trek to away games, and those who couldn't follow would listen for the scores on the evening news or local radio station. The year we made it to the state championship in Austin, a real estate sign was posted at the edge of town that read, *Last one to leave turn out the lights!*

The pressure could be high, but growing up surrounded by fanatics simply indulged and further enabled my passion to be in the middle of the action. There were some families whose lives revolved around the successes their children had as they switched from Pee Wee league football to middle school, junior varsity and then the varsity level. For those kids, the path was difficult. The pressure to perform from coaches and even fans could be suffocating, but having a safe haven at home, like I did, where effort was applauded more than results provided me the much-needed room to catch my breath.

Most of my teammates had the same thing, but those that didn't could find it at "Hawg meetings," where the big, thick offensive line would gather for dinner. We were dubbed by the coaches as "a bunch of hogs," or, as said in their thick Texas accents, "hawgs." Every Thursday night, Hawg parents would take turns cooking up asado for the whole team. It was a tradition that helped us get our minds ready for the big game the next day, but it was also just a good excuse to get together, eat and laugh off some of the pressure.

Had I decided that I was done with the dehydrating two-a-day football workouts or the monotony of running lines after basketball practice, my parents would have been content with my decision to walk away. If I chose to play, however, I had better go all in. Dad, an athlete in his own right, would spend his weekends and summer evenings pushing me to my limits in the weight room, simply by standing next to me and pushing his own. Mom was my number one fan and biggest cheerleader. Whether I was on the basketball court, the baseball diamond or stepping onto the football field, I knew with certainty that my parents would be perched somewhere in the bleachers on portable, padded Andrews High School branded stadium seats, cheering me on. Between the regular seasons of baseball, football and basketball, plus weekend tournaments and playoffs, I probably participated in hundreds of competitions. My dad never missed a single game. Mom missed only one, due to a work commitment, and I hit two home runs in her absence. She has yet to forgive herself.

THE FIRST BIG DETOUR

Transitioning out of high school sports and into college-level competition was a jarring wake-up call. For starters, playing varsity-level sports in Andrews, Texas, basically crowned me town royalty. At 6' 1", I had earned All-District, All-Permian Basin and All-Region honors. I was part of the student council and voted Mr. Andrews High School runner-up. In between practice for whatever sport was in season at the time and going to church every time the doors were open, my down time was never short on friends, and getting a date to the Homecoming dance wasn't difficult either. My eyes have been opened to the knowledge that my high school experience does not describe everyone else's—maybe not even most. The ease with which I was able to glide through those years is something I took for granted at the time, but now realize was an incredible gift.

During my junior year, I began to overhear news about scouts showing up to my games and then buzz about potential scholarships at major universities out of state. My future was laid out in front of me so clearly, it was almost as if I was physically watching as it took form. Playing college-level sports while I studied toward a career in coaching was what I had wanted since I was old enough to hold a bat. Every sweat-inducing workout, every game-winning score brought me one step closer to that dream.

But no amount of desire or commitment can make up for injury. In a comedy of errors, my senior year became filled with them, one after another, leaving me with a hurt back and turning me into a less desirable prospect for college scouts. Rumors of scholarships vanished almost immediately and my dilemma became not which university to accept, but rather if I would be invited to play at all.

Getting the call that I had made the roster for the baseball team at Lubbock Christian University was a game-changer for me, and one that would have seemed negative just months earlier. When I mentally hover above my past and see the arc of my story, I realize it was one of my defining moments. My dreams had been so specific, so detailed, that altering the narrative of my life in any way would throw everything else off course. When I gladly accepted that I would attend and play for LCU, a team that wasn't on my mental checklist of acceptable universities, I proved to myself that I could shift my expectations without compromising joy or my future. Playing college ball was only part of the dream. I wasn't walking onto a top-tier, Division 1 baseball program, as I had expected, but LCU definitely ran a respectable program. When I stepped up to the plate at my first game it was an overwhelming rush of satisfaction and adrenaline. My sports career had taken a turn I hadn't expected, and yet, I was still in the game. I had made it. I wasn't where I planned, but I was standing on home plate rather than sitting in the bleachers.

That euphoria didn't last long. If playing baseball in high school was fun, college turned it into a job. Which is fitting, I suppose, since in theory, college-level sports are supposed to prepare and train athletes for the big leagues. College didn't care that I was a big deal in my hometown. Mainly because all the other guys sitting next to me on the bench shared a similar history. Most of us left behind high school varsity teams where our names had been printed in permanent ink on the starting lineup. On our first day as freshmen, it became clear that even if we were big fish, we were now thrown into a vastly larger, more talented pond. I wasn't going to be the hero simply because I showed up. If I wanted playing time, my ability and my work ethic would have to match my ego.

I put in the work but didn't have much chance to prove myself at LCU before another injury forced my hand and I had to take a semester off for orthopedic rehabilitation and recovery. That period of rest was excruciating for me emotionally. I couldn't play baseball, so I watched it almost obsessively, desperate to get back into the game. The next season, despite my wrecked shoulder, Howard College in Big Spring listened to my sob story and gave me a shot at playing time. I was thankful that my college baseball career hadn't ended before it had a chance to really even begin, but my new coach tried my commitment in ways I hadn't expected. Howard College made LCU's baseball program look like a P.E. class. Baseball was no longer a pastime or a hobby I was highly devoted to. My new regimen demanded that I wake up at 4:30 to start my workout, breaking only for classes, and then wrap up the day at eight o'clock every evening with another workout or coaching session.

It was during the warm up for one of those Howard College games that I felt the pop. It was a simple throw, one I had done hundreds, if not thousands, of times before, but this time I felt pain tear through the muscle of my right shoulder as the ball left my hand. The pain was so intense and the pop so distinct that I knew, maybe even before the ball hit the catcher's mitt, that there was a possibility I would never play again. Sports had always come naturally to me. It was what I knew. There was no page in my story up to this point where it didn't appear. By the end of my second college season, my shoulder had finally deteriorated to the point of no return and rotator cuff surgery was now no longer optional. In one sentence, the surgeon pronounced an end to my baseball career, and to what I had been dedicating my life to for nearly two decades. It is bizarre to think how rapidly the road map for my future became filled with detours. So much of my identity had been wrapped up in my talent, in my on-base percentage and the prideful stride I got to make from the dugout to home plate. Walking away from the image I had spent a lifetime building was much more agonizing than the surgery that led to its end.

With nothing tying me to Big Spring now that the allure of making the team had faded, my future became a giant question mark. I had chosen LCU because it had chosen me. I didn't have any other attractive options out of high school, and moving to Lubbock meant I could play baseball through school while I got my degree, then start coaching and move up the ranks one season at a time. When Howard College gave me a shot no one else was offering, I took it without question. By taking baseball out of the equation, I now had options. Where did I really want to work and live?

Andrews, Lubbock and Big Spring had a lot to offer but scenery was not high on the list. My entire life had been lived against the backdrop of rolling tumbleweeds, thorny mesquite trees and dry creek beds. Continuing that pattern didn't sound too exciting. As I weighed my options, I knew the criteria for choosing my new school had simultaneously stayed the same and radically transformed. Baseball and sports in general were off the list for the first time in my life. Where they had always been unwaveringly at the top of my priorities in the past, now they were an afterthought. What hadn't changed: my ambition to become a coach. My destination was still the same, even though everything in between Point A and Point B had required a drastic alternative route.

Finding a beautiful campus that offered an excellent kinesiology program and wasn't too far from my Texas roots became the new litmus test. As I examined my options, I kept coming back to vacations I'd spent with my college roommates in the Texas Hill Country. During those trips, we had seen what Lake Travis and the surrounding area had to offer. It was beautiful, and filled with other college students my age. I convinced my roommate Ben to tag along with me to check out the area, thinking it could be the setting for our next adventure. We spent a few days exploring and looking at schools along the way. Before we left, we rented a few inner tubes and floated down the San Marcos River, near Texas State University. At the bottom of the waterway we climbed out of our rentals and onto the pier. An hour of drifting aimlessly on the water successfully cleared my head and made my choice clear. I grabbed the handle of Ben's inner tube, looked him in the eye as he scrambled up the ladder out of the water, and made my decision: "I'm moving down here whether you're coming with me or not."

HEARTBREAK HIGHWAY

The beauty of making plans is the optimism it implies. Plans are preparation for the future. As a high school athlete with an endless horizon of opportunities, the future was guaranteed. It was waiting for me, all I had to do was keep my head down and run toward my goals. College chipped away at that belief, but proved to me that I could take unexpected circumstances and disappointments and weave them into a full life. But the switch from playing baseball at the university of my choosing to playing baseball at whatever college would have me, is a minor-league disappointment. Earth shattering at the time as it was, it did not wreck me. And although I had to adjust my expectations, I continued to lay out mental blueprints for the future that, as far as I could see, were set in stone. I'm thankful for that naiveté. I don't regret my optimistic assumption that it would all work out in the end just as I had planned. Those hiccups, those minute glitches were preparing me, as they do all of us, to field the all-consuming waves that would eventually crash over and threaten to pull me under. It was a gift that I had no frame of reference for the heartbreak that lay ahead of me on a narrow stretch of highway or the pain that would make me dig deep to take the next life-giving breath in the ICU.

I see now that I was wrong: the future isn't waiting for me, at least not in the way I had imagined it would. I've seen too much, heard too much and lost too much to make plans in the same expectant way. I wake up every day in a body that experiences life in ways I could never have imagined when I was standing on home plate about to hit the game-winning home run. I shrug off the pain that greets me every morning, I choose to push back against excuses that everyone around me would accept as reasonable and then I carve out a life for myself in the midst of what others might view as ashes. I show up, but not for a future that fits flawlessly into a mold that requires everything to be perfect. I show up for today. I take what I have to work with at that very moment and I wring it out for every drop it's worth.

I no longer make plans. I make a life. It was a lesson I learned by almost losing mine.

At the plate.

3 BURNING DOWN

Paralysis haunted my childhood dreams. The situation and setting would change with the passing of each sleep cycle but the experience always remained the same. I would look up in my dream state to see a burning rafter hurtling toward me, but find that my feet were glued to the floor. If I could just jump I might be saved, but I was stuck and unable to move even an inch. Other nights I would be running away from something or someone chasing me and desperate to scream for help, but my voice was somehow switched to mute. I would grab at my throat and open my mouth wide but no matter how hard I tried, I couldn't make a sound. The dreams would roll and crash into my subconscious sometimes as frequently as once a week, plunging me in terror until I finally emerged alert and dripping with sweat.

In one distracted moment, the driver of a fully loaded cement mixer truck replaced those night terrors with a reality from which I would never fully recover or awaken. I had followed the rules: my seatbelt was clicked into place, my blinker was flashing and both of my hands were on the wheel. Two more seconds, hardly one breath's worth of time, and I would have turned left, away from the horror of being crushed almost to death by 33 tons of diesel, metal and construction materials; away from a lifetime of painful new truths. Trapped inside the burning remnants of the car I once spent Saturday mornings washing and buffing, it sunk in that this could be my finale. This would be where all of my stories, my years of studying and training, where my future would come to an abrupt halt: Tyson was a junior in college when he drove his Corvette down a two-lane highway in Buda, Texas, and was run over by a careless driver. The end.

There would be times in the days that followed when I would want to throw my head back and scream at the sky, "How dare this be my story!" Depositions would be given and investigations would be launched to determine how the driver at fault could have rear-ended me with such force that it overturned his massive vehicle and flattened mine beyond recognition, without offering so much as a pump of his brakes. A vortex of emotion would come later. But in those moments after impact there wasn't room for mental tantrums. My only focus was survival.

Swirls of black and gray surrounded me. I took shallow gasps, searching for oxygen through the thick blanket of smoke that now filled my car. With each second, heat pulsed and drew nearer like a bonfire out of control. I slammed the palms of my hands against the steering wheel and clawed at my waist in search of the seatbelt button, trying to break free. The world could have been on its side or upside down. I couldn't see the way out, but I knew an exit was likely inches away if only I could convince my car to release me. My screams for help echoed visceral and primal against burning metal and through dense billows of smoke that thickened as the fire around me churned. My throat strained against my panic. Terror rippled in tremors through my muscles as a harsh truth came to light: even if someone could hear me, any hope of rescue this far outside of city limits would not arrive in time for me to escape alive. Whether anyone else was sharing in my panic, I had no idea. My ears were occupied with one deafening sound: the roar of flames as they cracked and buckled the metal frame beneath me.

IMPACT

There were burned wires and blistering heat as the world around me melted. And then, in an instant, there was no pain, no sound, no light-rimmed tunnel. All I recall from the seconds after impact is terror, heat and the panic that accompanied my desperation to escape the car that was too quickly morphing into my grave. Beyond that, I'm left with an empty memory bank. I've since been able to fill in the details from eyewitness accounts, police reports and the medical team on the scene, but none of it is part of my personal memory.

Seconds before the cement mixer truck plowed over my car, then flipped onto its side and slid down the highway past me, Ryan Turner was avoiding interstate traffic by taking the same back road to a spring break vacation of his own. Packed into a Chevy pickup with three of his friends and the truck bed filled to the brim with camping supplies, Ryan watched as his friend carefully drove around me on the right, pulling off onto the shoulder for a quick moment before passing me and continuing on FM 1626. When he went around me on my right side, unknowingly avoiding a horrific wreck of his own by a narrow margin, the two girls squeezed into the front seat between he and the driver coincidentally turned around moments before the crash. Judging from the speed of the construction vehicle and the proximity of my car, they quickly realized what was about to happen. Their horrified screams made Ryan turn around just in time to see the collision unfold before him from just yards away. He watched as the violent wreck lifted my Corvette into the air and spun it around, before dropping it into oncoming traffic where it collided with a Nissan Xterra in the opposite lane. His friend saw it play out in his rearview mirror, then slammed on the pickup's brakes in response and threw the gear shift into park before all four spilled out of the truck and immediately began running toward the accident. The cement mixer, investigators would later determine, was going well over 60 miles per hour when it hit me. The momentum of impact pushed its massive weight up onto two wheels and then onto its side where it skidded across the blacktop and created a brief cyclone of sparks, metal grating against ground, before it came to rest in a ditch. While the other three passengers ran toward it, Ryan instead ran toward my car, which was now almost entirely engulfed in flames. He was the first person on the scene.

It's surprising how most everyday details evade us, and yet some are etched into our lives forever. Ryan couldn't tell you what he ate for breakfast that day, or what he and his friends were talking about just moments before they passed me on that old stretch of country back road. And yet, the minutes surrounding impact remain crystal clear for him. As he ran from the safety of the pickup, he began making out images through the suspended particles of dust, smoke and rubble that hovered between us. His stomach tightened as a dark red lump on the pavement drew closer with each step. In those moments, he recalls, he was convinced he was about to walk up on a severed body part at worst, a puddle of spilled blood at best. The impact had been so fierce, so loud, that he was certain I was dead, or at the very least, victim to what would have to be a gruesome, body-mangling scene. As the red image came into focus, he was relieved to discover the comforting sight of a maroon Texas State University baseball cap, a hat he was used to seeing daily on campus as a student there. We were peers. And although before this moment we had never met, it is chilling to imagine how many times we must have passed each other in class, at restaurants, and on campus sidewalks completely oblivious to the knowledge that Ryan would one day run into danger to risk his own life for mine.

I have no memory of Ryan in those seconds after impact, but he and I spoke as I sat trapped in the midst of flames. As he approached me, I caught his eyes and yelled, "You have to help me get out of here!" Ryan jumped into action, grabbing me underneath my arms and lifting. My body remained wedged. At 130 pounds, he assumed his strength wasn't enough match for my then 210-pound, six-feet one-inch frame. He began scanning the side of the road for help and spotted a man sitting in the ditch nearby whose large build Ryan knew could make the difference in freeing me. He screamed at him, begging for help but the man never even looked in his direction, suffering from what Ryan would later assume was shock. As he looks back on that day, Ryan ironically describes that moment as his own dream of paralyzed terror. He screamed for help, knowing it was only feet from him, but none came. It was as if no one had even heard him.

90 SECONDS AFTER IMPACT

While Ryan looked away toward the roadside to ask for help, I twisted my torso around and began pulling myself up using the driver's seat headrest. My whole being was on autopilot at this point, simply doing anything possible to escape the flames. In that moment, two men in white button up shirts, ties and dress pants appeared through the smoke, seemingly out of nowhere.

Daryl O'Neal and Phillip Breedlove had been on location at Plum Creek Golf Course with a client for ESPN Radio that morning. As they made their way back to Austin, Daryl decided they should take FM 1626, a shortcut he became familiar with growing up near the area, to avoid a traffic jam on Interstate 35. Entering the school zone for Elm Grove Elementary, they saw dust and fire churning in the air. As they passed the school, they could see a car on fire about a quarter of a mile up the road. Daryl remembers thinking to himself, *Oh, God, please let there already be 50 people there. Where is EMS?* Being a first responder, he recalls, was his worst nightmare.

Phillip slid the car into park in the opposite lane, and the two threw their doors open, leaving the car to idle. The secondary wreck with the Xterra, which occurred when my car was lifted into the air upon impact and thrown into the adjacent lane, had blocked both directions of traffic, shielding them from other drivers. As they ran toward me, my upper body flailed as I screamed for help. My Corvette was now nothing more than a black metal frame, disfigured to the point that it was unrecognizable. Daryl approached, unable to tell which end had been the hood and which had been the bumper. The image of me hysterically screaming and waving my arms at him while in the middle of a firestorm still doesn't make sense to Daryl. Viewing the crumpled car around me, he couldn't believe I had survived to this point. Instead, he remembers a car submerged in flames and what he describes as "a kid that had just been poked down into this mess."

When they joined forces with Ryan to rescue me, it became clear that Ryan had been unsuccessful not because of my weight, but because my feet were entangled underneath the dashboard. Freeing them was not as simple as reaching down to untie a knot or cut wires. Each second that passed meant inches gained by the overwhelming heat and flames. Getting close enough to the scorching metal car frame to unravel the wires around my feet would be impossible without protection.

As if out of an action movie, Phillip grabbed the handle to the Corvette's passenger-side door that now lay strewn in the wreckage along the asphalt. Using it as a shield, he fought back the flames long enough to reach the tangle of wires that refused to release me and pried my feet loose. Together, the three men raised me out of the burning chaos—one lifting upward at my armpits, the other two tugging against my belt and pant legs. In unison, they began taking steps towards the grass nearby, mentally battling the importance of keeping me immobilized and removing me from what had become an extremely unstable situation. As they took careful steps, the mood shifted. My body, which seconds earlier had been writhing and screaming for help, went limp, silent and pale.

The three carefully lowered my lifeless body onto a strip

of grass, just beyond the dirt that separated the road from the neighboring lawns. At the exact same moment, as though choreographed for film, an explosion pushed them forward and sent a burst of smoke and flames shooting into the air. The hair on the back of Ryan's neck bristled and he looked down to examine himself. His pink Abercrombie T-shirt and khaki cargo shorts were damp with sweat but his flip flops were soaked. Phillip, Ryan and Daryl stared at each other speechless as their shared reality sunk in. They had all been standing in a spreading pool of gasoline.

THREE MINUTES AFTER IMPACT

When the unmistakable sound of metal twisting into submission as it ground against earth echoed down FM 1626, it caught the attention of everyone within earshot. Neighbors began pouring out of their houses to stand in front lawns, one hand clasped over their mouths in shock that something so horrific had interrupted their mid-day schedules.

Less than a mile up the road, Elm Grove Elementary School's parking lot had been buzzing with the hum of students and teachers as kids toured emergency vehicles for Fire Day. At the alarming sound of the mixer truck barreling over my sports car, the members of the Buda Volunteer Fire Department instinctively knew that what had just occurred would require specialized help–and fast. Transitioning intuitively from education to rescue mode, they radioed for backup, specifically in-flight paramedics who could arrive much more quickly to our remote location than an ambulance could, and filed into the trucks to drive toward us.

As the explosion continued to roar behind Ryan, Phillip and Daryl, heat shot toward them in warning flares until they reluctantly decided it would be in my best interest to move me again, this time to a safer, shady spot a few feet further along the road, rather than risk another larger blast or the rapid spread of flames to our nearby refuge of gravel and grass. I was still eerily quiet and unresponsive. My skin had turned from pale to an even ghostlier shade of white. Seeing my condition deteriorate so rapidly would be confirmation to them as they later drove away that my survival was surely an impossibility.

Mercifully, the volunteer firemen pulled up, followed by police, sirens blaring. Water hoses were rapidly unrolled to address the car fire while other professionals took over for Ryan, Phillip and Daryl, assessing my condition and hastily trying to stabilize me.

Within moments the recognizable rhythm of propellers dwarfed the crackling growl of the steaming wreckage as a STAR Flight helicopter descended and landed on the yellow dotted lines, surprisingly close to the accident. An emergency medical team poured out of the chopper, bringing with them a gurney, medical kits and mobile crash cart in rehearsed procession. Together they began to pelt Ryan, Daryl and Phillip with questions in rapid-fire sequence.

"What happened?"

"Do you know this guy?"

"Where's his backpack?"

"Who are you?"

The exchange from lying in the grass to loaded on a gurney ready for takeoff took place so quickly the action almost appeared blurry for onlookers. Daryl would later describe what he witnessed in the two minutes the helicopter was on the ground as "a badass cavalry." As quickly as it appeared, the helicopter lifted and took off towards Brackenridge Hospital.

After I was airlifted and out of sight, Ryan, Daryl and Phillip stayed only long enough to answer questions from the police. As the immediate trauma of what they had just endured began to erode, it became apparent that none of them wanted to talk about what they had just been through and seen.

The narrow two lanes were now filled with people. Each had arrived in layers: Ryan and his three friends and Phillip and Daryl first, rescue personnel second, and behind it waves of passersby and inquisitive neighbors. Curiously, those who witnessed the most wanted to discuss it the least. As the layers who had arrived third and fourth stood on warm pavement or freshly trimmed yards, and leaned against parked cars blocked by the remains of the wreck, Ryan, Daryl and Phillip nodded silently at each other, got back into their vehicles–still parked crooked with engines running–and drove away.

TWELVE MINUTES AFTER IMPACT

A few miles away, Amber was heading home from work and calling my cell phone. Something wasn't right. Our daily ritual, which consisted of me calling her at the end of her shift, was missing today. In the months leading up to this moment, I had never missed a phone call. Her stomach tightened as her mind wandered to places she feared. Her phone rang but the familiar voice on the other end of the line belonged to her dad, not me. A neighbor, oblivious of the connection, had seen the wreck and knew it would cause a nuisance for her parents when they commuted home that day. Her dad, hoping to spare Amber the same headache as she drove to their house that afternoon, called her cell phone unaware that the wreck he was explaining would profoundly affect all of their lives. For Amber, his phone call simply reinforced what she feared. When he heard the shudder in her voice and the possibility of what waited on the road ahead, Amber's dad begged her to turn around.

The stoplight ahead of her turned red but she knew braking was not an option. If I was fine, I would have called. I would have been taking that exact route just moments ago. Something had happened to me.

THIRTEEN MINUTES AFTER IMPACT

I woke up fighting. Nothing was clear other than the surge

of panic that renewed as I gained awareness. I thrashed and grabbed at tubes and wires coming out of my body until a man's face came into focus, inches away from my eyes. J.R., the flight paramedic, chose to speak complete honesty to me, a choice I believe kept me alive for the remainder of the flight.

"Sir, if you don't let us help you, you're going to die. Focus on one breath at a time."

My hands went slack as I tried to inhale. Blackness encroached on the corners of my vision and I once again slipped out of consciousness.

FIFTEEN MINUTES AFTER IMPACT

As she crested the small hill of FM 1626, the enormity of the wreck washed over Amber. She drew a sharp breath and held it before her lungs forced out the air in a painful heave. The sight could only be described as grisly. Smoke lingered in a wide halo above while firemen near the edge of the commotion began to wrap up unnecessary hoses on a second truck. Siren lights spun deafeningly silent. She drove onto the shoulder, away from traffic that was being rerouted, parked her car and took wobbly steps toward the scene.

People were everywhere. Extra patrol officers began getting in their cars, dwindling in numbers as the initial commotion and dust settled. Neighbors she knew by name congregated in driveways, unaware of how close to home this tragedy had struck. For one long second, the circulation of smoke and people shifted, revealing charred asphalt, then my Corvette's remains. Where my car had been almost unrecognizable to my rescuers, Amber knew instantly that it was mine. The crushing weight of this new truth collapsed her legs beneath her and she fell to her knees, sobbing.

Time did not stop, of course, but sound seemed to disappear for a moment, as the movements around her occurred in slow motion: the remaining police huddled together chatting as they made notes and examined the scene;

the firemen who slammed shut doors and turned off valves, preparing to leave. A collective burst of sound then rushed back like one giant exhale as life returned to normal speed. She stood and ran toward the squad cars.

"Where is he?"

"What happened?"

She asked trembling questions through tears but was met only with sympathy and short prepared answers they had no doubt given hundreds of times in similar situations.

"Is he OK?"

No answers. Only, "Ma'am, I'm sorry but we can't release any information to you at this time."

"IS HE ALIVE?!"

She spun around, searching for answers and spotted one of the firetrucks about to drive away, unnecessary now that the wreckage had given way to a smoldering ash. In movie-like form, she sprinted ahead of it, turned around to face the truck and stood immovable in its path. It stopped. Her questions spilled over again, this time with more force and through gritted teeth.

"WHERE IS HE?!"

"WHERE IS TYSON?!"

One of the firemen leaned out the passenger side window and tilted his helmet back, his familiar face coming into view. Amber's breaths choked in the back of her throat as the face of an old friend from school stared back at her. Her shoulders loosened as the combative tension she had prepared fell away, and she stepped to the side to look up at him.

"That was your boyfriend's car, wasn't it, Amber?" he asked.

She nodded, tears streaming down her face and onto shoulders that now shook. He took an exaggerated breath and looked off into the distance, as though considering whether or not he should continue.

"They took him to Brackenridge Hospital. They've already had to revive him four times. That's all I can tell you. I'm sorry."

He leaned back into his seat and the truck accelerated. She watched as it left her behind, taillights bouncing, while it climbed the hill and then disappeared. Her eyes slowly took in the remnants of the scene around her. She stood motionless, on the side of the road and alone.

A secondary wave of grief and fear began to build as she slowly reached for her cell phone. My parents, miles away in West Texas, had no idea what had just happened. It was now up to her to tell them.

Hy Road and the school zone speed limit sign.

The 33-ton cement mixer on its side.

Phillip, Daryl and Ryan look on while emergency personnel prepare me for STAR Flight transport.

The cavalry loading me onto the helicopter; Phillip and Daryl's ESPN Radio SUV parked in the ditch.

My Corvette on the left, and the Nissan Xterra.

Burned, crushed and twisted into scraps.

4 TRAUMA UNRAVELING

It was not a good day for a crisis. No day is, of course, but March 11 was especially inconvenient for my family. Every minute of my parents' day–sunup to sundown–had already been planned and scheduled. Family from all over had begun caravanning to their new home in Midland, Texas, where a baby shower to celebrate my nephew Austin would take place the next day. Not only would my parents host a crowd of family and friends for the party, but they'd also be feeding and housing extended family for a long weekend. My mother was beside herself cleaning, cooking, decorating and readying guest rooms for family that would begin arriving later that afternoon. My aunt Karen was on the road from Snyder and had almost arrived at my parents' house when my mom heard the phone ring. She picked up the cordless phone from the kitchen counter and balanced it on her shoulder as she folded a kitchen towel.

"Hello?" she answered, turning on the kitchen tap to rinse cups in the sink.

No answer.

"Hello?" she asked again.

Hysterical laughter rushed at her from the other end of the line. Her hands paused mid-air, water spilling onto the counter as she tried to make sense of the jumble of noise. There was something in that sound she recognized.

"Amber?" she asked. "Is that you?"

The voice heaved, then wavered, unable to speak. It wasn't laughter she had heard, but a mixture of moans and screams.

"Martha…" Amber half-yelled to my mom through stuttered breaths. "Tyson's been in a really bad accident."

At those words, my mom says, the room began to spin. Meal planning, wrapping presents and setting out centerpieces dissolved under the weight of Amber's cries until all that remained was terror and questions.

"Amber, what happened?! Is he OK?!"

From her roadside view and with that one sentence, Amber had shared all the information she possessed. As they exchanged muffled sobs over the phone—my mom a five-hour drive away and Amber so close to the carnage of my wreck that her hair would smell of burnt rubber, smoke and spent airbags when she finally made it to the hospital—they shared a heartbreaking reality: neither one knew how badly I had been hurt, or if I had survived at all.

LIFE AS SHE KNEW IT

Farm to Market Road 1626's tangle of metal debris and onlookers was beginning to slowly unwind. The wreck would not be without consequences, but a fatality was thankfully not one of them. There were only two other victims involved, the driver of the Nissan Xterra, who suffered a broken nose, and the driver of the cement mixer, who was taken to the hospital with an injured back but was released later that evening. After the three of us were evacuated by ambulance and helicopter respectively, the focus shifted to clearing the highway and allowing traffic and life to return to normal. Amber, however, had not moved from the shoulder where she stood when the firetruck pulled away minutes earlier, leaving her with the only information she would learn for hours: my injuries were critical, I had died and had to be revived four times before being loaded onto a STAR Flight helicopter, and I was being taken to Brackenridge Hospital. It was the small square of land, a spot that she had driven past hundreds of times before, from where she had placed the life-altering phone call to my parents and, moving forward, would be the literal and symbolic road marker for the beginning of her own painful journey.

Driving towards University Medical Center Brackenridge was the next step, but even as she stood, she felt her whole body involuntarily shuddering. The drive toward downtown Austin would, at best, take more than half an hour. If traffic was especially congested the trip could top out at over an hour. Shock had gripped her, taking over her emotions and stability, but it had not clouded her judgment. She stared through a filter of tears at her car, still wedged into the ditch nearby, waiting for her decision. Driving herself would not be an option, but neither was standing still.

IN THE WOODS, NOT OUT

Trauma unit specialists stood ready as the helicopter landed at University Medical Center Brackenridge. J.R., the flight paramedic, and his team led the rapid conversion from transport care to hospitalization, briefing on my injuries as they rushed me inside, then slowed to a rehearsed walk as they released my gurney into the hands of staff doctors and nurses.

My appearance was misleading. There were no blood-soaked bandages to peel away, no disfiguring gashes to address. Astonishingly, I was neither bloodied nor burned. There were no head wounds or lacerations to apply pressure to, but my ghostly pale complexion implied what my untouched external concealed. I was unconscious for this transition, but the speed with which I arrived on the operating table leads me to believe there was little if any hesitation during their assessment of my situation. I was wheeled to the operating room in one continuous motion to confirm what the STAR Flight and trauma teams already knew. No one could see it, but I was, in fact, bleeding.

As they pushed past double doors into the surgical unit, I woke up briefly, bobbing at the surface for awareness. During those muddled few moments, I didn't sense any pain, only a brightly lit room, mouthfuls of foreign medical jargon and what seemed like hundreds of medical professionals buzzing around the room and peering over me. Then the room went dark as anesthesia pulled me under again.

The first cut was a hurried slice from the base of my right armpit along the entire length of my right shoulder blade in one large half-circle. Planned and scheduled surgeries leave careful, straight, small wounds. Cuts incurred in the trauma unit are impulsive and tend to be jagged and large, as mine was, requiring more than 30 staples. The scar I now carry with me is a lasting reminder of how close I came to death that day. There was no small area that could be carefully searched through laparoscopy. All of my internal organs were a crap shoot. Which one was bleeding, which one was no longer functioning, which one could, essentially, kill me if not repaired was unclear until that first incision. Although neither my parents nor I have any regrets about the decisions made in the operating room that evening, the surgeon would later apologize to my parents for the lengthy uneven scar when they happened to step onto the same hospital elevator a few evenings later. "I knew he was bleeding," he told them remorsefully. "I just had to get in there."

While I lay unaware in the surgical unit, Amber arrived at the hospital, driven by a neighbor who was home at the time of the accident. He pulled up to the hospital entrance and paused, realizing the magnitude of what she was about to walk into by herself. But an audience, she knew, would only intensify her pain. She shook her head at his offer to stay and stepped out of the car. The automatic doors opened on cue, and she put her hand over her mouth to soften the sound of her uneven breathing while she frantically searched for the emergency room check-in desk. The afternoon waiting room around the unit reception area was unusually empty.

"My boyfriend was brought in by STAR Flight…" She tried to steady her faltering voice. "He was in a wreck. His name is Tyson Dever."

The clerk clicked and typed, then confirmed that I had indeed been brought in and was in surgery. Asking for information beyond that confirmation brought another round of the same phrases said in the same sympathetic, yet firm, tone she had heard an hour earlier: *I'm sorry, but we can't release any information to you at this time.*

She was the first one in the family to learn of my wreck, and the first one to arrive at the hospital, but without my parents present, she would be treated like a stranger. She walked, tunnel vision, to an empty area of the waiting room and collapsed into a worn vinyl chair. Announcements garbled through the intercom and a television on mute glowed reruns in the corner. Bouncing her eyes along the empty hallway nearby, she wondered where I was in the hospital, and if I was still alive. The last two hours didn't make any sense. She reviewed them again and again in her mind, trying to understand, but there were no answers or reasoning, only silence.

Down the hall, my first surgery was complete but my body was not responding as doctors had hoped. My blood pressure would not stabilize and my heart was racing; I was bleeding internally, but from where, they were uncertain. During the exploratory surgery, doctors discovered multiple broken ribs which had punctured one of my lungs but could not be responsible for the amount of internal bleeding I was currently experiencing. With my condition deteriorating, the medical team rushed me back into the operating room for a second operation. This one began with a small incision below my belly button and continued six inches across my abdomen where doctors inserted a scope to determine which organ was causing my body to sound an alarm. Through the search it became apparent that my diaphragm had been torn upon impact and my abdominal cavity was rapidly filling with blood as a result of trauma. After addressing the trauma and sealing the tear, the scale of my recovery began to tilt in a positive direction. My heart slowed to a more sustainable rate and my vitals began to stabilize. The surgical team breathed a sigh of relief, proud they had solved another puzzle, and wheeled me to a curtained-off room in the Intensive Care Unit where I would be closely monitored. My body had proved it was willing to recover, but I was not out of the woods yet.

THE LONGEST, QUIETEST DAY

Back in Midland, the moment she set the phone receiver back on the counter, a new schedule was put in motion for my mom. She steadied her voice with a shallow breath, then dialed my dad, who had gone to the gym earlier that day. As was his habit at the time, he left his cell phone in the car. No answer. She then dialed my aunt Karen, and in a matter of minutes, the two remapped the day from manicures and laughter between sisters to transferring all hostess duties to my aunt Karen for the remainder of the weekend. Although Karen was willing to do whatever my mother needed at that moment, she would later tell her that putting on a smile for guests and playing hostess while I was in the hospital fighting for my life was the hardest thing she had ever done. My mom placed another call to her brother Herman and then began frantically trying to book a flight to Austin. The drive from Midland to Austin would take about five hours but, like Amber, my mom knew neither she nor my dad would be in any condition to drive.

An hour later, my dad slid back into his truck and picked up his phone to find 32 missed calls. Cell phone technology in 2005 was not nearly as advanced as what we're used to today. Voicemail wasn't standard and texting and caller ID weren't the norm. The cell phone my dad carried was for work, and few people knew the number. So while 32 missed calls raised a flag of concern for my dad, of course, it did not send him into a panic, either. The calls could have been a mistake, a wrong number.

When he arrived home and my mom broke the news, it seemed impossible to him. Dad and I had spoken on the phone at two o'clock, just as he was leaving to go to the gym and as I was headed towards Amber's parents' house in Buda. He immediately dialed University Medical Center Brackenridge but they relayed a similar phrase Amber would hear for hours on end: *I'm sorry but we cannot release any information over the phone.* The only news they would share was that I was in very serious condition. In his stunned state, my dad assumed I couldn't be injured beyond a broken leg. I would recover, he told himself. He just needed to get to Austin to check on me.

The earliest flight out of Midland to Austin was at 7 p.m., three hours later. Grief and uncertainty settled over my parents as they stuffed clothes into luggage. How do you pack for a trip you desperately hoped you'd never have to take? Making their way to the airport, and then to the boarding area of their terminal, they began what my mom calls The Longest, Quietest Day.

Once they left for their flight, I'm not sure either of my parents spoke another word until they landed in Austin. No one spoke to them either, in part, my mom believes, because their faces were so grave and full of despair. In the Midland airport, my mom sat despondent, staring at the wall, at the floor, out the window. My dad, full of nerves, paced in circles around food kiosks, through rows of predictable airport seating and at gate entrances. On the plane, where he was forced to sit, he stared at the floor, with cold chills rattling down his neck and spine. His mind rolled over and over how he might fix this for me. As a dad, he would tell me later, you always fix whatever's wrong. This, he knew, he couldn't fix.

THE WILL TO LIVE

It was just after 8:30 p.m. when my parents finally stepped

out onto the hospital sidewalk. Guided by bright parking lot lighting that drew moths flying in circles through the evening air, they took the same heavy steps through automatic doors that Amber had taken hours earlier. The information they had managed to receive over the phone offered my parents little more than they already knew. I was in surgery. No one knew my progress. No one knew if I was alive.

It had been only hours since my parents received word about my accident, but a lifetime had passed. They raced to the floor where I was recovering, but every leg of the trip that brought them closer to me felt more sluggish than the last. Now they were only steps away and my mom felt like the world had slowed down around her. Elevator doors, nurses, custodial staff–no one and nothing was moving fast enough.

When they made it to the nurses' station, it was not during the allotted visitation times that are strictly enforced by the Intensive Care Unit staff. At the distress on my parents' faces, the doctor made an exception, and gave his approval for them to slip into my room, but only for a few moments. I would still be under anesthesia from my second surgery, he told them, but I was stabilized and they could at least be in the same room with me, if only for a minute.

As they followed the doctor down the ICU corridor, past doors that opened only upon scanning hospital security badges, they realized they had no idea what they were walking into. The doctor hadn't detailed what the surgery was for, what he had operated on or what my injuries were. They readied themselves emotionally for what they might see. Tubes, beeping monitors and IV bags that hung near my bedside were accessories they knew would come with ICU territory, but my appearance was a question mark. Was I missing limbs? Had I been injured or burned so badly that they wouldn't be able to recognize my face? What about my eyes, my hands? Would I even know who they were?

As they walked into my room they were stunned at what they saw. My face, my mom recalls, was "perfect." Later we'd discover two small burns–one on top of my knee and one behind my leg–and a gash that removed a small portion of my right ear. This was actually a gift. My right ear had always oddly been larger than my left; now they would be even.

Beyond those minor imperfections and a few insignificant scratches, my skin was free of scrapes or bruising. My undamaged appearance made the countless number of tubes and wires attached to my body seem ridiculous and unnecessary. How I had been entirely run over by a 33-ton truck and lived to tell the story is remarkable, but emerging from the wreck without external evidence of trauma was miraculous. As my parents stood over me weeping and speaking softly to me, my eyes fluttered open briefly in recognition of their voices. The doctor had given them no information so far, except to say that I was completely under and would not be responsive or awake during their short visit. The comfort and familiarity of their voices drew me out from under the weight of anesthesia. It was only for a moment, and one I don't remember, but it gave my parents the reassurance they needed to know that although my body was under siege by a trauma we could not have anticipated, I was still there. Between the heavy cloud of their grief and the blur of medicine that held me back, our eyes met, and my parents knew I would be OK.

The doctor who conducted my second operation entered the room and cut their visit short, citing my need to rest. Together they retraced their steps down winding hallways as the surgeon gave them a brief update on my condition. My injuries were significant. He recounted how my broken ribs had played a part in my punctured lung, how the bleeding had gone unaccounted for in my abdomen after the first surgery, requiring the second one which stopped the hemorrhaging and addressed my torn diaphragm, and explained the next steps: MRIs, X-rays and constant monitoring. Before they passed through the final locked doors that separated the ICU and public waiting areas, he paused, placing his hands in the pockets of his white coat.

"I've been doing this for 30 years," he told my parents,

"and this boy had the strongest will to live I've ever seen. That's what saved his life. He was bound and determined to live."

The doctor pressed the exit button, opening the double doors for them to exit through, and walked back toward the hallway of patient care rooms. Now that they had seen me alive, the cumulative exhaustion of the day unleashed its weight onto them, but the relief they felt allowed some of the day's trauma to unfurl off their shoulders. I had a long way to go, but would survive. It was the answer to an agonizing question left unspoken between them as they paced in airport terminals, sat impatiently on tarmacs and fidgeted against seatbelts. For the first time since the phone rang at 2:45 p.m., my parents took a breath.

The hospital walls glowed white against the ever-present fluorescent lights. It was now well after dark, but the night shift was just getting started. Nurses flipped through charts and technicians rolled carts down hallways, greeting them with quiet nods as they passed. There was nothing more they could do. Hours of anguish as they tried to reach me had ended. Now began the waiting period and its own unique brand of sorrow.

They turned the corner towards the waiting area then stopped, overwhelmed by their view. A standing-room-only crowd of family and friends had gathered, hoping for good news and anxious to encourage my parents. As they entered the room, they saw faces representing different walks of their life–church friends, a few of my old teammates, family members who drove long hours to only sit for a few moments–the mixture of people was astonishing. Although their connections to our family were each unique, their emotions were all identical, mimicking the anguish, worry and fear my parents felt and displayed.

My mom took a seat by the waiting room desk so she could be near the hospital phone, ready to receive news about my condition and field the already overwhelming number of calls streaming in from friends and relatives as news of my wreck gradually trickled through social circles. If my wreck were to occur today, my family would have lots of options, like blog posts, social media updates or even specialized sites like CaringBridge, which would allow them to provide updates on my condition all at once. In 2005, however, those options weren't as common. My mom spent most of those first few hours and the days that followed on the phone, reliving and recounting the details over and over again to concerned friends and family. The support was overwhelming and buoyed them in those early days, even though she was unable to return every call.

True to form, my dad alternated between standing and pacing. The strict visitation hours in the ICU meant only two family members would be allowed in my room every four hours, and only for 15 minutes at a time. Since the doctor greenlighted my parents' quick check-in outside of regular visitation hours, it would be less than two hours before they saw me again. When you're in the midst of a crisis and a hospital waiting room is your headquarters, however, the minutes tick by glacially. Having family and friends there to literally surround my parents was a gift we will never forget.

I LOVE YOU

At 11 p.m. my parents rushed back to my room, refusing to waste a moment of their anticipated 15 minutes. The nurse reminded my parents of my status. Tubing in my nose and mouth would prevent me from speaking, but the anesthesia's strength would likely prevent me from even being aware of their presence. A few more hours and they could expect to have an opportunity to interact with me. They pulled up chairs next to my bed and began to softly talk to me, repeating to me what they had been repeating to themselves throughout the evening: "Tyson, you're going to be OK."

The sound of their voices flipped a switch somewhere deep in my mind and engaged my senses. My eyelashes tugged against each other, reluctant to allow my eyes the privilege of opening. The seconds passed thick and slow as shapes began to take form around the room. Two squares above me glowed distorted and fuzzy until I cleared the water slowly from my eyes with long blinks, revealing dimmed incandescent fixtures surrounded by matching white ceiling tiles. With each breath, my eyes involuntarily shut, as though the act of seeing withdrew more energy than my body could offer. Still frames from the previous hours dragged sluggish and opaque across my memory. As one Polaroid flashed, another would appear behind it.

There was asphalt. Miles of asphalt. Then heat that made my skin prickle in remembrance.

I took thin breaths in synch with the beeping machinery nearby, each one drawing attention to the discovery of a new injury. My sensory capabilities began throbbing, coming back to life and making me less aware of my surroundings but more in tune with the pain coursing through my body. There were tubes everywhere—between my lips, in my nose, and countless lines that draped from both sides of my body to the edges of the bed where they disappeared. My throat chafed against tubing as I tried to swallow.

Although I was awake, I could feel my body slipping back into sleep. My eyes opened in slits, hungry for information, and scanned the room until the faces of my parents, visibly exhausted even in blurred form, came into view nearby, their faces red and swollen with worry. Although I was the one in the hospital bed, I could see I was not the only one injured. Their emotional pain added a new dimension to the physical pain that threatened to swallow me whole. Drawing on strength I did not have, I lifted my left arm towards them and made the sign for "I love you" with my hand. They both began to cry. Then the world went dark again.

My 22nd birthday. Three months before my wreck.

5 BROKEN UP AND
IN HALF

Waking up on day two after my accident was different than my brief, but groggy, wakeful moments throughout the night after my surgery. Anesthesia's narcoleptic effects were now gone and the barrier it created between my consciousness and pain had worn to a thin layer of separation. Upon waking, a nurse came in and explained my morphine pump, demonstrating how pressing its button would send pain reliever through my IV. But even morphine quickly reached its limitations. As my pain level escalated, the nurses would respond to my call button and sheepishly tell me that, yes, my morphine pump was still working, but I had reached my maximum allowable limit for the time being.

Losing the anesthetized buzz also made the tubing and attachments throughout my body noticeable with every breath or slight movement. Soon after becoming alert, the medical staff compassionately obliged my requests to remove the tube that trailed from my mouth down my throat and had kept me breathing during my intensive surgeries. Shortly after, the NG tube that was inserted through my nose, past my throat to reach my stomach, was removed as well. Other attachments remained for days, including tubes on either side of my body that drained fluid from my lungs. Had I known how painful removing them would be, I might have considered leaving them in as really awkward accessories for the rest of my life. After a week's time, my skin made a primitive attempt to close the wound itself and grew onto the tubing. Without any anesthesia or numbing medicine, they were removed in one quick motion. It was two seconds of horrible, breathless agony and the worst pain I felt throughout my entire recovery.

I was now awake but exhausted, so while the long four-hour stretches between visits were isolating, I was not lonely. Had I been in charge of my own schedule, I would have allowed visitors every moment of my recovery, and the nursing staff quickly figured this out. I wanted to see the room full of friends and family that had gathered just down the hall, but the staff's unshakeable ICU visitation rules stood in the way, creating a barrier I wasn't wise enough at the time to enforce myself. I desperately needed rest to heal.

It was a relief every four hours to watch my parents and Amber alternately push past my ICU curtain to sit by my bedside. As I gained more awareness I asked more questions but answers were not easy to come by. My parents didn't have much information about my diagnosis because the doctors weren't ready to make any declarations. Inflammation in my body was rampant and an accurate MRI would be impossible until the swelling settled down. Law enforcement proved to be a dead end as well. The investigation was ongoing, but police had no obvious explanations for why the driver of the cement mixer slammed into me without leaving a single skid mark from his brakes. The only thing we knew for certain was that I was alive, sitting in the same room with the people I loved most, breathing the same air.

At the end of 15 minutes we would have an uneasy, quick goodbye and I would watch them leave, fluttering the same curtain as they stoically walked away, arms and legs stiff from worry. Seeing their pain was worse than the torture of each breath through my punctured lung and torn diaphragm.

One night as we were about to part for another four-hour stretch, I stopped my dad with a casual question.

"Hey, Dad." My voice faded in and out, still weak from intubation and pain killers. "It's so strange. I can't wiggle my toe." Dad paused at the foot of my bed, his hand resting on my foot through the sheets. His head tilted as he tried to make sense of what I had just said. "I keep staring at my big toe," I explained, "but I can't get it to move."

My parents both shrugged off my comment nonchalantly, relaying what the doctor had told them: I had an enormous amount of swelling in my spine and my immobility was probably a side effect, but we'd know more after the MRI. Excruciating uncertainty and fear had been coursing through my family in the hours and days since my mom answered the phone call that changed her life. Out of necessity, she and my dad had developed an incredibly convincing poker face. Every second in the ICU waiting room was filled with terror and panic but they never once shared those concerns with me.

From the outside looking in, being unable to move any part of your body is alarming. It's a giant red flag warning that something has drastically changed. Stress had wrapped itself so tightly around us that I'm not sure any of us could grasp the severity of my injuries at that point. We were so focused on our gratitude–I had survived!–that we were numb to the possibility that more bad news could be waiting around the corner. What we had already endured was so horrific, we convinced ourselves that the worst was behind us.

But as they left, it began to creep into my thoughts that maybe swelling wasn't what kept my toe from responding. What if it was something more?

FOR BETTER OR FOR WORSE

Twenty-four hours passed before my doctors were willing

to try an MRI. Waiting didn't accomplish what they had hoped and the swelling from my injuries continued to make for an unsuccessful, unclear scan. To move forward in the right direction with my recovery, the type and extent of my spinal injuries needed to be understood, so a minor surgery was ordered to investigate the condition of my spine with a scope and small incision. What we thought was an exploratory mission was actually our doctor's final point of confirmation, deeming his suspicions fact: my spine had been severed.

My dad was the first to hear the news. It's an unusual type of burden to be handed information that holds the power to crush the ones you love most. As you receive it, the pain it inflicts is terrible, but the real agony comes from knowing you've been chosen to hand it off to someone you love and witness their pain as well. He filled the two hours during the surgery doing what he had done for days now. The waiting room clock ticked especially loud as he paced back and forth, picking up a magazine only to set it back down. Mom had taken a rare moment away from the hospital to accompany Amber to a doctor's appointment. During those early days, no one ever really left the hospital. There were mini-walks around the parking lot for fresh air, or rushing to the hotel for a hot shower, but that was about it. An orthodontist appointment seemed so ridiculous in the face of what they were all enduring, that Amber planned to cancel, but my mom insisted she keep it.

"It's a 10-minute appointment," I remember Mom saying to Amber. "It's OK; I'll go with you. It will get us out of the hospital."

After surgery, with me still under anesthesia, the doctor stepped into the waiting room and called out my dad's name. They shuffled to a deserted corner nearby.

"Mr. Dever," the doctor started, "I went in and scoped his back. His spine is severed. There is a one-inch gap between his vertebrae and his nerves. There is no attachment whatsoever. It's a complete break."

My dad stood frozen and felt the blood drain from his face and hands until they turned cold. No other words have weighed heavier on my father's shoulders than the sentences spoken in that dim hospital alcove. He blinked, trying to process this revelation spoken so bluntly and practically. The words equaled the outcome they feared most, second only to my death, and it was relayed so frankly, it was as though he was listening to the doctor read his dinner order off a menu. Our optimistic outlook had betrayed us all. What we blamed on swelling was actually a completely ravaged spinal cord. The impact had literally broken me in half. There would be no U-turn. This was our future, for better or worse.

The doctor continued to detail to my father what he had seen during the operation.

"His nerve endings are mangled. They look like raw hamburger meat that has been in the microwave for too long. There is nothing to attach together."

Sensing my father's next question, he answered before my dad could form the words.

"I can't tell you he'll never walk again," the doctor said without emotion. "As a doctor, I would say he has a one percent chance, just to give him hope. But on a personal level, I can tell you, no, he'll never walk again."

There was a pause then, "Do you have any more questions?" My dad shook his head half-heartedly, lips parted, unable to produce words or string them together. The doctor turned on his heel and walked away quickly through the corridor until he disappeared down one of the maze of hallways. My dad stood still and breathless—the new bearer of bad news.

"IT WAS RIPPED FROM US."

My mom's phone rang as Amber signed in at the reception desk.

"Hello?" she answered.

She was quiet for a moment and then raced out the

doorway of the orthodontist's office to the parking lot. There she folded over the hood of Amber's car, her shoulders quivering in sobs, her voice howling through cries that sounded more like screams.

Amber rushed out to follow her and put her hand on her arm, trying to make sense of what was happening. Mom tried to breathe, to gasp for air to speak, but the emotion was too big. She looked up at Amber and knew she now had to pass on the pain that had been handed to her. With shaking hands, she reluctantly delivered the answer they all knew was possible, but didn't dare entertain as likely.

"We hung onto that last hope," my mom would say months later when we were finally able to speak of those early days. "We hung on, but it was ripped from us."

MY BIGGEST REGRET

In two days' time, more than 50 people had come to the hospital to see me. It was frustrating to me that there was a room full of people, some who had driven hours to visit, whom I would be unable to personally speak to or hug. It was the beginning of a frustrating list of things I would be unable to do.

On Tuesday, day four after the accident, the permanence of my future was made official. I remember the moment that all of the pieces clicked into place and the truth about my injuries was revealed. My exhausted mother was sitting in the chair next to my bed. She had found a hotel near the hospital the night of my accident, but it had basically become a place to keep luggage and shower. I'm not sure she slept at all those first few days. If she wasn't by my bedside, she was returning the hundreds of phone calls that kept her cell phone and the hospital waiting room phone incessantly ringing.

Every four hours we'd have the same conversation: "Mom, am I going to walk again?"

Her reply was always the same heartfelt refrain, "You're doing good, Tyson. You're going to be all right."

We played out this routine about ten different times before she finally collapsed into the truth. I knew the answer, but somehow hearing it from someone I trusted, someone who knew me better than anyone else, was an important part of acceptance for me.

From my mother's perspective, focusing on staying positive was her way to protect me from something that was outside of her control. She couldn't stand in front of the cement truck and shield me from this new reality. She couldn't don surgical gloves and fix my wounds. She couldn't take away the pain that stabbed with each breath or the restlessness that came with being held captive in a hospital bed. What she could do was guard my spirit. The doctors were focusing on my physical wounds but as my mother, she was aware of how my emotions and attitude could affect my recovery. She was terrified I would slip into depression or begin a downward spiral that would hinder my physical progression toward healing.

As I look back on that moment I realize my questions were selfish. I wish I could've understood what life was like for her on the visitor side of the hospital bed. I wish I had been strong enough to accept the answer without forcing her to give voice to the painful news that was already crushing her spirit even as she smiled back at me.

"No, Tyson," she said softly, her voice catching. "You're not going to walk again. You're paralyzed. But it's all going to be all right."

If I could change anything about that week of my life, it would not be the accident. I wouldn't reverse my diagnosis. My life has changed in radical ways so that every detail of my day is different, but it's who I am now. It's part of me. I've more than accepted it; I've embraced it. I wouldn't change this future that was created by a careless act. Instead I would enter back into that moment, when I was lying in the hospital bed, full of uncertainty about the future, and I would take back my words. I would not make my mom answer that question. I would not make her respond to a question she should not have had to hear. No mother should have to tell her child he will never walk again. It is my biggest regret.

Watching the faces of my parents in that moment was a turning point for me. I could see, then more than any other moment in my life, that my response would directly affect their well-being. Would I wallow? I was certainly entitled to. Yes, they were accountable for their own actions and emotions, just as I was in control of my reaction, but this was a different ballgame. It was entirely up to me whether I increased their burden and deepened their suffering, or lightened their load and brought joy into the situation. It was one powerful act in the midst of excruciating powerlessness.

My parents stared motionless, quietly analyzing my face while they waited for my reaction. I glared at my big toe frozen in place, a still-life portrait of a body that had played varsity football and made the college baseball roster.

"That's OK," I said. "I'll just play wheelchair basketball."

BOBBING FOR AIR

As I stabilized, my recovery needs switched from staying alive to learning how to live. Sooner than expected, I was transferred by ambulance to TIRR Memorial Herman, a rehabilitation hospital in Houston. Although I would be there for rehabilitation rather than survival, inpatient rehab meant 24-hour care, so the setting appeared much the same. I would be surrounded by the same endless panels of beige wallpaper and sleep each night in a hospital bed, but this round of treatment had a purpose: to guide me closer to independence and freedom. When the ambulance doors opened in TIRR's parking lot, my stretcher was carefully lifted out and steered through a labyrinth of hallways and elevators. This was a new sensation I had yet to get used to: being carried, driven, and pushed where I needed to go. I entered rehab a passenger. The goal would be to leave as the driver.

I stared at the squares of incandescent lighting that strobed overhead as we passed one after the other until reaching the floor designated for spinal cord injuries. There my room consisted of a handicap accessible bathroom with a shower I could roll into, a bed, privacy curtain and a bed for another patient. The experience was much like being blindfolded, driven across the country and dropped off with a wave and "Good luck!" Rehab, I soon discovered, was the process of removing the blindfold, getting my bearings and finding my way home. There would be occupational therapy, which would teach me how to independently perform daily tasks like self-care, and physical therapy, which addressed my physical ailments and overall health. Over the course of three months, I would spend a total of six weeks there learning how to live within a body that was now a foreign object to me.

Each morning started with an insane amount of unknowns, with my personal goal being: Just get to the end of each day, for crying out loud. As I progressed from the basics, like how to shower independently, my goal changed to: Get to whatever normal is going to be as fast as you possibly can.

The first three weeks left me fairly limited in what I could attempt because of the back brace that protected my still fresh spine stabilization surgery. We lovingly nicknamed the hard-plastic enclosure Turtle Shell, mainly because it looked like one, but also because the recovery process kept us in an inescapable state of seriousness and we had to find humor where most people couldn't. Even when some people might deem it inappropriate, laughter prevented the nerve endings of our emotions from being deadened by stress. If we wanted to come out on the other side of this with any semblance of ourselves, we needed to throw off tension whenever possible.

I loathed the morning routine of those first few weeks. Every day a nurse would walk in before breakfast carrying a breathing tube and a sympathetic smile, knowing what was to come. I would blow into the tube as hard as I could, for as long as I could, to ward off the pneumonia that wanted to settle into my battered lungs and inactive body. It was only one breath, but forcefully exhaling with a punctured lung, torn diaphragm and countless other internal bruising and injuries was, to put it mildly, less than pleasant. Once the breathing tube was behind me, whatever the rest of the day held for me seemed doable.

Movement toward my new normal was slow and painstakingly difficult. I have a memory of lying in the ICU, a few days after gaining full consciousness, and asking my mom if it was OK for me to raise my head off the pillow. My spinal column had been so damaged that I was unsure what was allowed and what was off-limits. Lifting my head wouldn't have caused further harm, but I wasn't too far off base. Rehab was a one-day-at-a-time process requiring hundreds of meticulous baby steps. We had to protect me from further ravaging my body, while balancing the need to get me moving and independent again.

During those first sessions, rehab was done in my room. Eventually I would be allowed to go to physical and occupational therapy rather than having it come to me, but to go, I had to get there, and getting there meant wheels. To live the life of independence I craved, becoming mobile was priority one, but it would not be easy. I had to learn how to transfer into a wheelchair, how to propel myself forward and how to balance through it all. But first, I had to learn how to sit up. It was another simple task that could no longer be taken for granted.

Scared is probably the best way to describe how I felt as I transitioned into a wheelchair from my hospital bed for the first time, a few days before being transported to TIRR. Three doctors and nurses came into my hospital room and cautiously sat me up in bed, steadying me and my cumbersome back brace supports. Sitting up as a paraplegic for the first time is akin to bobbing in a lake without knowing how to tread water. As I sat on the edge of my bed, legs dangling over the side, it occurred to me that not only could I not feel my legs, but I also could not feel my butt. I sat inexplicably floating, unsure if I was still secure on the bed or had been lifted by the medical team surrounding me. The process of moving from bed to chair at this stage of my recovery would be dangerous, so nurses positioned a slide board, reaching from bed to wheelchair, like a tiny, awkward playground slide. I readied myself for my first transition and listened as they explained how I would depend on my arm strength to determine the speed with which I slid down the board, but reminded me that they would be carrying most of the load for me.

The room began to swirl. Sitting up after having languished in bed for so long triggered a physical response in my body. Beads of sweat appeared on my temples and forehead, and goosebumps rose on my forearms. As I battled nausea and my gag reflex, the doctors flanking me explained in medical terms that the sudden onset of pain I was experiencing was known as symptoms of autonomic dysreflexia, and, if left to intensify, could be life-threatening for me. Medically speaking, it meant my body suddenly experienced an extreme spike in blood pressure. In layman's terms, my body was responding to pain it could no longer feel. Although I have only encountered the full-fledged disorder twice, I still get vague feelings that mimic the pain I felt that afternoon. If I stub my toe or put my legs into bathwater that is too hot, I can't feel the actual pain, but my body still responds in alarm through instant nausea and sweating. Some view it as a curse, but it's at the very least a necessary evil for me; without it, I might burn my legs or injure my foot and have no idea until a simple inconvenience turns into a minor injury or worse.

The medical team repositioned me to allow my stomach to settle and my body to calm while I strained to reset my focus. The slide board sat under my legs, and I tried to decipher where to place my hands to remain stable. Little by little, inch by inch, I scooted with the help of nurses and doctors into the wheelchair until I sat, floating, on wheels. It was my first moment of freedom since I heard the last few click-clacks of my turn signal on 5 Mile Dam Road.

My reward was a brief trip outside hospital walls. The medical team pushed me out of my room, down the hall and in and out of elevators until we reached the first-floor exit where a few of my buddies had gathered outside to congratulate me. We hung out for a while, like we always had, and I turned my face up to the sun I hadn't seen or felt in weeks. It is amazing how differently you experience fresh air when you've been without it for an extended amount of time. Even if my lungs had been fully recovered, I couldn't have taken in as much air as my body was begging for.

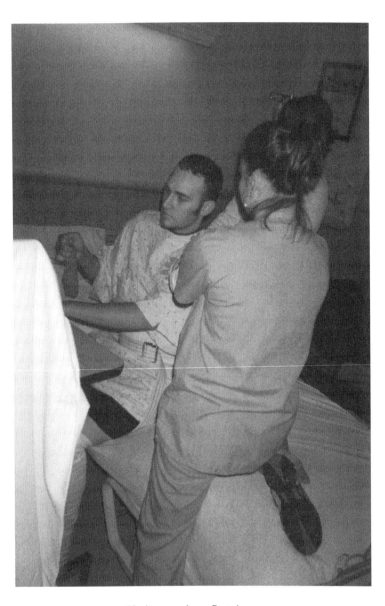

Sitting up but floating

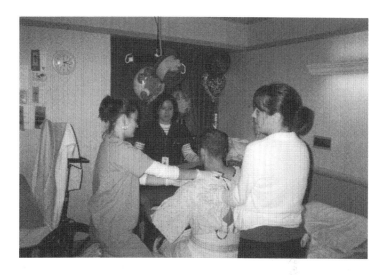

Sitting up in bed for the first time as a paraplegic. Look closely, and you'll see the slide board in the wheelchair nearby and the jagged scar on my spine fresh from surgery.

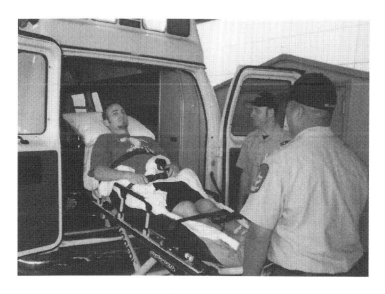

Transport to rehab at TIRR by ambulance.

6 MY SECOND LIFE

It was now the doctors' agendas and their assessments of my recovery and progress that decided how much freedom or pain relief I was allowed. I couldn't go for a ride up and down the hallways of the unit or a quick bite to eat in the cafeteria. I couldn't even get up to use the restroom by myself. Machines beeped in chorus with each other around the clock so that the tune of morphine drips and pulse ox alarms became the soundtrack of my life. When I hear those sounds now, whether on a television show or in an actual hospital, I'm transported back to those early days and the humbling feeling that comes from being at the mercy of other people's choices. My independence had been taken from me. Days before, mere hours earlier, I had been running sprints and lifting weights, walking to class and driving to work. Now I was a prisoner of the hospital and of my own body's limitations.

When you train yourself to live a life that pushes boundaries, it is unbearable to wake up one morning in a body full of them. Never in my life had I come across a physical obstacle that I couldn't fix by simply pushing harder, getting stronger or working longer. That wasn't an accident. My dad had made sure that perseverance was ingrained into me from the day I was old enough to throw a baseball. Unlike the kids on my team whose dads were only involved enough to scream from the bleachers, but not to play catch in the backyard, I was fortunate to have a father who took deep pride and interest in my successes and was willing to do the hard work to get me there. It wasn't long after my first little league game that Dad became my own personal trainer and off-season coach.

For my dad, being fit wasn't something he took on because of me, nor was it something that waxed and waned depending on the season or his workload. Hitting the gym was a necessity for him, then as it is now. When I was in high school, he would come home from work around 5:30 in the evening, change and head straight to the gym without fail. His commitment was an inspiration to me, but it also held me accountable. My dad, in his forties at the time, had worked all day and was headed to the gym. Why wasn't I? I usually couldn't find a good enough excuse to skip and spent most afternoons alongside him, watching as he put men younger than him to shame.

Our routine was steady: one hour of weights in the gym—legs one day, arms the next, then chest—before heading to the bowl-shaped Andrews High School football stadium where we ran up bleachers, our quick steps echoing across the metal stands, or up the steep, sloped sides of the arena. We would fight each other for the lead, our backs dripping sweat in the dry west Texas heat, then walk back down and do it all over again. In between races to the top, we chatted through water breaks about football, the upcoming season, what was going on with school, girlfriends and sports. The hours we spent playing catch, practicing drills and training in the gym and on the field became a cornerstone for our relationship as father and son. I deeply respected his work ethic and strength, although his stamina and expectations sometimes pushed me further than I felt I was capable. When he pressed me to run faster or be better, I wanted to dig deep and prove myself because I couldn't stand to let him down. Sometimes I failed, but when I met the lofty standards he set for me, it was a natural high that kept me coming back for more.

I relied on his training during every practice and every game. With his guidance, I had thrown myself into baseball, football and basketball, and wrapped my identity tightly around my physical abilities. Just a few days earlier, that trait had been a gift.

From the constraints of my hospital bed, I let my brain wander through the glory days of my strength, how my legs could somehow muster the brute force needed to climb hills and outrun competitors. I stared at fluid drip slowly into my IV until my eyes glazed over, my mind beginning to outline a program that would lift me over these new hurdles and help me get back to life as usual. Dad's words echoed in my mind, "Come on, Tyson. Faster!" My hands clenched instinctively in determination as my head spun with ideas. Maybe I could beat the odds, I thought. I inhaled sharply, breath burning against the injured walls of my lungs, as a harsh new awareness rushed in. My plans were worthless in light of new revelations. The doctor's diagnosis played on repeat in my ears: "He'll never walk again." My grip loosened and my head fell backwards in defeat against the scratchy hospital-grade pillowcase.

Spinal cord injuries that result in breaks fall into one of two categories: complete or incomplete. The difference is drastic. A complete break offers a dismal chance of regaining motor and sensory capabilities, while an incomplete one offers a much more optimistic outlook. My T-12 vertebrae was shattered and my spinal cord completely severed. This race was already lost. I couldn't work or train my way out of it. I was lying in a body riddled with restrictions that no amount of effort would ever overcome. I stared at empty walls and tubing that draped from IV pole to arm and wondered, Should I ever look forward to life again?

The sterile walls seemed to draw closer and closer every day as I lay trapped in bed. Some days left me in a morphine fog, others gave me too much space to contemplate this new, uninvited chapter in my story. During those sluggish hours, I had plenty of time to consider how I would handle this new existence. I could check out of my own life; no one would blame me. There were people who would care for me and provide for me for the rest of my life, I was sure. My parents would move heaven and earth to make sure I had a place to stay and my basic needs met. It's an uncomfortable truth, but I remember wondering if I even wanted to continue at all. So much had been taken from me. Did I want to live the life I had now? Even if I could figure out how to do life without legs, did I want to? I could shut down and end the pain and the frustration. I could internally fold up, become smaller and let others do the heavy lifting. After all, who would expect me to pull my own weight? The first few days were not bleak. To the contrary, I remained startlingly and excessively positive. But it would be a lie to say that I was not faced with the task of sifting through dark, heavy options to uncover the right ones. I was the champion in my story and my own villain at the same time.

Others would always be more uncomfortable with my new existence than I personally felt, and visits from friends and hospital staff in the early days after my wreck were a preview of that awkward new inevitability. Merging their bonds with me pre- and post-wreck would leave most people at a loss. It became clear to me that most people saw me as having two lives: the first carried me around on legs, the second did not. And I understood their dilemma. This new experience was unsettling, and merging those two identities didn't make sense to most people. At first, I felt in synch with their approach to the new me. It was tempting to separate my memories into categories, labeling them with mental notes of Life 1: with legs and Life 2: without. Or as some viewed me, Life 2: with boundaries and Life 1: without.

But as I spent hours staring at legs that wouldn't budge and willing them—begging them—to move, I found a turning point. It was so blatantly obvious that it seemed almost silly that I hadn't been able to grasp it earlier. It became the new tagline I mentally repeated when the stack of things I couldn't do anymore began to teeter and threatened to topple me.

The mantra was simply this: I'm still Tyson. My legs just don't work anymore.

That motto was the key that unlocked the door to a new outlook for me. When I took hold of that belief, it became clear that my entire identity would not be from the victimization of my wreck. I still had the same goals, the same sense of humor and the same optimistic spirit. Most importantly, I had the same fight and drive that my dad instilled in me through sports as a child and that doctors told my parents had saved my life against all odds.

My life would be different, but it was not over. I needed to live like it.

NO MORE NORMAL

My situation was oddly both grim and optimistic in the early days of rehab. My complete spinal break meant my chances of walking were essentially nonexistent, a crushing memory that surprised me every morning as my eyelids warily raised to discover the permanence of what I assumed had been a horrifically real dream. In the midst of it all, somehow, learning the tricks and skills I needed to live independently became strangely satisfying. Each day's grueling schedule of therapy meant I was one day closer to getting back to whatever rearranged version of life awaited me.

As my life changed, my body changed as well. Over the few weeks I spent in the hospital, my body rapidly shed weight. My calves, which I had spent years bulking up through weight lifting and resistance training, now shrunk to nearly half their size. By the time I was lifted out of the ambulance and rolled into rehab, I had lost 60 pounds.

My legs were not the only muscles that began to atrophy. My lower core and abdominal muscles had also been affected and could no longer be depended upon to create balance or equilibrium. My top two abs, shoulders and arms would now be in charge of keeping me stable and upright.

My lower body didn't necessarily have to atrophy, my therapists confidently explained one day during a session. Regaining tone in my leg muscles could be possible, but it would not be done through traditional exercise. Instead, therapists would essentially shock my unresponsive muscles through the power of a TENS unit and electrodes attached to specific muscle groups. Historically, a large percentage of paraplegics like me experienced that, although they could not feel the movement, their limbs could respond to the current and push stationary bike pedals or even walk. The hope was that this electrotherapy would protect the integrity of my legs, allowing me to retain some muscle, even though I was unable to use them on my own.

I was cautiously optimistic as the therapist peeled paper backing from each electrode and strategically adhered them to my legs. I watched as she pressed different buttons and turned dials trying to get the intensity just right while keeping an eye on my movements. My eyes darted back and forth between her facial expression and my legs which sat rebelliously indifferent. She adjusted a dial, then pressed the button again. Nothing. Again, she turned the dial, sending a higher level of electric current jolting painlessly through my muscles. Nothing. To her credit, she genuinely wanted the treatment to work for me—so much so that I eventually developed a burn where the electrodes had been placed. My reputation for being a medical marvel—surviving a wreck that should have ripped me apart, and exhibiting a will to live that baffled my doctors—continued, but this time in a way that wasn't in my favor. Although many people with injuries that matched mine had at least some level of success with the TENS unit, I fell into the rare group of patients—a tiny percentage—who had no benefits. Having an unsuccessful experience with the TENS unit therapy was insignificant in my overall recovery, but it confirmed the fate of my appearance. My once powerful legs were now strikingly small, and having no response to the TENS unit meant that was how they would remain.

While I was in therapy sessions, my mom and Amber attended classes within the rehabilitation hospital, where they would join other family members navigating the same unfamiliar territory. Spouses and parents of patients would file into classrooms for tutorials on things that were previously givens, but would for the foreseeable future represent a challenging part of all our daily lives.

Interactions with other families living on the spinal injury floor of a rehab hospital provided an odd microcosm of people who would have normally never crossed paths, but were now all thrust into a similar, unwelcome experience. As I mastered the ability to get in and out of my wheelchair, we would roll down to eat lunch or dinner in the cafeteria in between therapy sessions, a welcome break from the monotony of my room. At shared tables, we interacted with other families who had endured the same upheaval as us: a man left paralyzed by a random shooting, a veteran learning to walk with only one leg, a man in his twenties, who, for an entire year after his own wreck, received no professional care for his resulting paralysis because his family was without insurance and couldn't afford specialized treatment. It was a unique comfort zone that allowed me to test the waters of this new life while surrounded by people who dealt with the same wounds, both emotional and physical. We had all checked our judgmental attitudes at the door, and now sat in the same mess together.

At times throughout my stay, that camaraderie extended to my roommates as well when the second bed in my room was filled by another patient. The most memorable was Mitchell, a high school kid who was left paralyzed from the waist down after a freak dirt bike accident. He lit up the room with laughter and cheerfulness, and we bonded over a shared football rivalry between Oklahoma University and the University of Texas. He had arrived at rehab before me, and was weeks ahead of me in his recovery. His physical progress gave me healthy motivation, but it was his positive approach to the experience that helped calm me and allowed me to get more comfortable in my own skin.

We were throwing friendly football trash talk back and forth one evening when Mitchell decided to reheat some pizza slices leftover from dinner. He grabbed the cardboard pizza box, tossed it onto his lap and pushed against the rims of his wheelchair as he disappeared out the door. In the small kitchenette of the shared lounge area down the hall, I could hear him pressing buttons on the microwave as he warmed a piece for himself and for me until the cheese bubbled from the heat. A few minutes later he rolled back into our room, pizza steaming on thin paper plates balanced on his lap. Our trash talk picked right back up where we left off while he set the pizza onto the adjustable hospital rolling table next to me. As the plates lifted, bright red oval burns on the tops of his thighs came into view. We fell silent as we took in the injury he could not feel and hadn't been able to notice. After a long pause, Mitchell tried to brush off the burns as no big deal but we both knew a call to the nurses' station was a necessity. We took a few silent bites, lingering in a moment when we were just two guys, short-term roommates, eating leftover pizza. But reality couldn't be silenced. Injuries would be different now and so would preventing them. Normal was no longer normal. Never before had I considered that placing a hot plate on my lap could burn me. It hadn't happened once in my first life. But this was my second life, and I had so much to learn.

WILL YOU MARRY ME?

In the hours, days and weeks after my accident, the people closest to me–my parents and Amber–heard the same thoughtful words over and over. Sometimes they would come in different forms, but the words usually carried the same aim. People would put a hand on Amber's and say, "I'm so sorry. I'm here for you." She would smile and nod, glossing over her own misery in order to avoid amplifying others' discomfort. Internally, however, she was boiling with resentment.

How? How are you here for me? she would silently scream. *You don't feel what I feel. You don't understand the pain and hurt that settles in when someone who means so much to you is going through something like this and there's nothing–nothing–you can do.*

It was a general feeling of helplessness that followed our relationship from the ICU to recovery, rehab and then outpatient care. She was tireless in how she fought for me. Most nights, she slept on the sofa or cot by my hospital bed while her days were filled with learning how to bridge this new reality together.

After outpatient care, I lived temporarily in her family's enclosed garage, which, with my parents' help, they had overhauled into an incredible handicap accessible mini-apartment. During the day, Amber would work two jobs and then at night she would come home and help me continue my rehab and take care of my battered body. It was during that time, with her family's willingness to help and because of Amber's devotion, that my recovery really gained traction.

There was no stone left unturned when it came to her relentless search of ways to best support and encourage me. The title of "girlfriend" just didn't carry enough weight for the commitment we had to each other, for the lifetime's worth of pain, emotion and heartache that charged at us in a span of mere weeks.

When I proposed from my hospital bed a few days after my accident, it was both spontaneous and premeditated. I had already made the decision to marry her, but our timetable had shrunk. It was now obvious that life was no longer limitless for us. The wreck had exposed how easily we could be broken and how quickly everything could vanish. It was as though we had fast forwarded to the future and suddenly we were hypersensitive to our mortality. Our youth would not be endless; my current state had proven that. Every moment that passed with Amber sitting at my bedside, flanked by beeping monitors that signaled whether I would live or die, felt more urgent than the last. Waiting for weeks or months, a time when life would be back to "normal," no longer seemed like a viable option.

When I asked and she said "yes," I believe we both meant it. Our "yes" was different now though. We weren't saying "yes" to the future we expected, and, as we soon realized, our futures were not the only ones disrupted. There were other participants who had been dragged into this new heartbreaking version of our story along with us, and as we would discover in the subsequent weeks, their emotions would have just as much impact on the longevity of our relationship as our own.

When you've endured something as horrific as my accident, support is a critical element to recovery. As you progress through the healing process, different types and forms of help and encouragement make all the difference. As support rolled in after my wreck, I imagined everyone I knew–friends, family, co-workers, school acquaintances, old teammates–lined up, arms locked around me in concentric circles. The importance and intensity of those relationships increased as the layers drew nearer to me, positioned in the center, resembling rings of support around me in the shape of a bullseye. As phone calls spread across state lines, through family members, then neighbors and old friends, help poured in. People in the outer rings sent cards filled with encouraging words and checked in by phone with my parents. Interior rings made visits to the hospital, used the key under the mat to pile foil-wrapped meals in our freezer, mowed my parents' lawn and made sure newspapers didn't disintegrate on our driveway, forgotten. At the center, in the innermost ring, my family and Amber were there to hold things together when it all seemed to be falling apart. I was extraordinarily fortunate to have such crowded inner circles.

As the extent of my trauma became clear, both emotional and physical, the circles around me stood firm, engulfing me in support and love and daily self-sacrifice. The weight of our shared burden pressed heavy on all of our shoulders, but those standing valiantly in the circles nearest me felt its strain the most. They were the ones who carried our shattered pieces for us until we could attempt putting them back together again.

Our circumstances continued to bear down on us, and over time, muscles quivered, nerves frayed and emotions ran high under its weight. No one's support wavered, not even for a moment. I never once woke up and felt alone. I never doubted that the future would hold the same family unity as it had before. But even so, there was no denying that this future would be drastically different. The love that had cinched Amber and me together through months of recovery and rehab began to chafe against this steep learning curve. We found ways to connect that felt familiar, like ice cream dates, concerts and movie nights. I could no longer open the door for her, but she would sit on my lap and I would push the rims of my chair to get us where we needed to go while she laughed and called me her "free ride." We were still us, but no amount of shared experiences could erase the raw pain our families endured as a result of our mutual heartache and its exhausting aftermath. Trauma is a team sport. The moment my car was annihilated and my body forever transformed, those standing in the inner circles felt the aftershocks of the impact, too. The alterations to my life would be most obvious, but it would be unfair to deny that they would also be permanently affected. Their futures shifted, and their dreams and plans changed, just as mine did.

The day I packed up my belongings and moved out of Amber's house and into an apartment away from her was one of the most difficult seasons of my life. Leaving was the right thing to do; we decided that together. It was painful, of course, but giving ourselves the freedom to acknowledge that the future was no longer as clear cut as it had once been allowed us room to see more clearly. Stress had created a fuzzy haze that enveloped and protected us from looking too far into the future. In the early weeks, it served as a life preserver, rendering Amber and me unable to look beyond the next hour or day and focus only on that moment's achievement of survival. But as weeks turned into months, the fog began to lift. We looked into the lifetime ahead and realized it was not the same dream anymore. To someone peering in from the outside, it may have looked like failure. To us, it was a bold win. We were willing to take brave strides away from a future we no longer wanted, while wading through an ocean of suffering that made us want to cling to what was comfortable. Not everyone can muster the same courage.

It was love, not duty that kept my parents and Amber at my side for the months-long process of learning to live again. It was an unglamorous daily grind of small victories and they came back every day for more. The dedication required to walk through this type of valley with someone is difficult to relate to others because there is very little in life to compare it to. There is no time off, no weekend break, no guarantee in the distance that it will get easier someday. I will always have this traumatic life-shattering mile marker in my past. The minutiae of life that we all do without thinking–getting dressed, going out to eat, unloading groceries–will require focused effort for the rest of my life. I had a lengthy list of people who were willing to march beside me as I learned how to move forward and there will never be enough ways to say "thank you" for their immeasurable love, encouragement and help. But as the dust settled and this new life began to take shape around me, I realized I had a decision to make. One that only I could choose. It would be the ultimate deciding factor for everything and every choice that followed: Did I want to be the victim in my story, or the hero? I know it was because of the unquestionable support of my inner circle, Amber included, that I was able to make the right choice from the moment it was presented to me.

As I licked my wounds in the days that followed our cancelled engagement, my parents were incredible pillars of strength. I remember how embarrassing and heartbreaking it was to share the news of our breakup with people who hadn't yet heard the rumors and it seemed like I was having to do so on repeat. I was reliving the awkwardness of it all with a family friend one evening when my dad, seeing my discomfort, leaned over and whispered in my ear, "It's OK. You were on a lot of morphine in that hospital. You proposed to me, too."

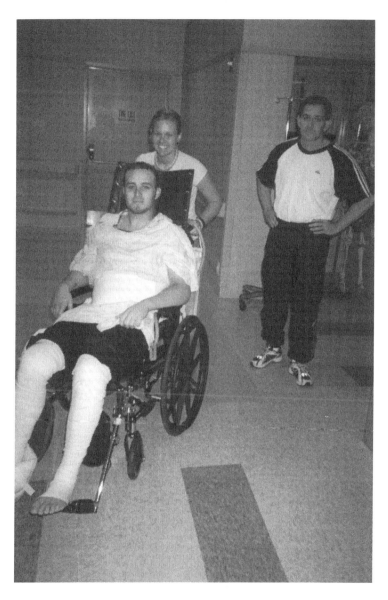

Amber pushing my wheelchair; my dad in the background

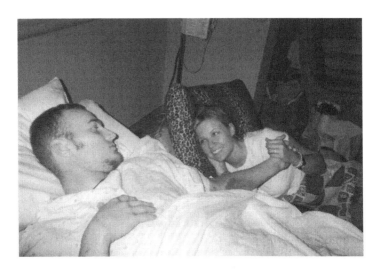

Engaged.

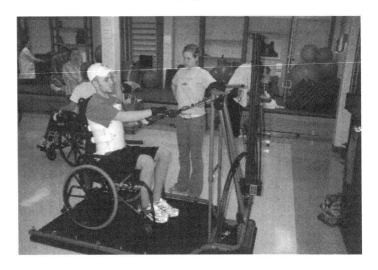

Working out in rehab with Amber.

PART TWO: ROAD TO RESCUE

7 HILLTOPS AND VALLEYS

"I spent six weeks in rehab" is something I love to casually slip into conversation. It usually sends a raised eyebrow or two in my direction, and at the very least, delivers an awkward pause. There are other ways to say I had to power through inpatient physical therapy and rehabilitation for weeks at a time, of course, but catching people off guard is one of the guilty pleasures paralysis allows me. Most people step and speak so carefully around me, like I'm fragile or easily offended simply because I'm in a chair. When people are extra cautious around me, it sends the message that I'm small, feeble and incapable. It says, whether they mean to or not, that they underestimate me. By their actions and words, I can see they have no idea how much emotional muscle, grit and will power it took to overcome the earth-shattering changes that life placed in my path. It's the reason I make (slightly inappropriate) jokes like:

You know what's the best part about being in a wheelchair?
You never have to buy new shoes.

I'm stronger than they think. Humor is the best way I've

found to remind them.

I wasn't trying to wean myself off of drugs or alcohol through a 12-step program, of course, but like an addict, rehab for me had its own necessary steps. As I look back on those challenging weeks, now years later, I can see how those steps didn't only apply to my life inside of rehab, but outside, too. In fact, it's possible that my mental and emotional rehabilitations were more challenging, and maybe even more important, than the physical healing that took place. When I arrived at death's door, it was an opportunity to sort through and name the steps I had been following all along to get through tough times. As magnified as the choices behind each step became because of my wreck, I've been pleasantly surprised to discover that the steps I found to repair a broken body and spirit have endured beyond the hospital walls. I still apply them to my life on a daily basis.

I had an unfortunate front-row seat to watch other people in my same position who struggled and–heartbreakingly–gave up. For whatever reason, they couldn't harness their own inner strength once the outer strength left. My survival does not make me superior, and recovery must be customized, but I realize now that there were action steps that could have made the difference for them. In the midst of my own personal disaster, it was these three steps that I relied on to put power back into my hands in moments when it felt as though it was being stripped away.

STEP 1: LIFE IS HARD. DEAL WITH IT.

My wreck was an absolute, total train derailment for me. I was going on a spring break vacation. I was a year away from a college degree. I was working long hours doing something I loathed to save up money for a future doing something I loved. The next step seemed so obvious and so tangible to me that I could almost picture myself on the football field or the baseball diamond, calling my team to huddle so I could deliver the final pep talk before a big win.

It added insult to injury that I had done nothing wrong to bring about this drastic course change. My driving had been absolutely textbook in that moment: my seatbelt was on, my blinker was flashing, and my hands were at ten and two. The radio wasn't blaring; I wasn't on my cell phone. I had done nothing to deserve this. And yet, here I am. This would now be my truth. I mentally reviewed my options during my first three-week stint in rehab. Ending it all or tuning out, I had decided, were not acceptable choices for me. Rolling up and down the hallways of TIRR during my final session revealed that not everyone was strong enough to choose that route. Some of my fellow patients were not able or willing to muster up the resolve it takes to look fully into the mirror, wheelchair and all, and be excited about tomorrow.

It wasn't so much that I wanted to survive as much as I desperately didn't want to just exist. I wanted to be independent and strong and do things for myself. I wanted to push forward with my career aspirations and get back to doing the things I loved. I wanted to climb aboard a fishing boat and cast a line while the sun was still rising. I wanted to push past brush and mesquite trees as I hunted deer and dove. I would not sit in this chair and watch my life rush by just because my legs didn't work. I refused to give up.

That refusal meant acknowledging a gut-wrenching, brutal truth: life is going to be hard, and I have to decide to be OK with that. Every day I make the choice that even if life is a 180-degree directional change from what I expected, I have the ability and the drive to make my life one worth living. Even if the driver of that cement mixer had pumped his brakes in time or swerved off the road and missed me, life would still be difficult in other ways. As long as I'm breathing, life will throw its curveballs at me, often when I least expect it. I don't have to be on death's door to find myself in a position where I need to press on in the midst of tough situations. Every day means a new challenge, and a choice: either give up or deal with it. I'll choose the second one every time.

STEP 2: STOP FEELING SORRY FOR YOURSELF.

After I asked myself, *Do I want my life to end over something that wasn't my fault?* I also had to pick where I wanted to place my blame. Of course, the man who was so distracted and irresponsible that he was driving 30 to 40 miles over the speed limit in a school zone before nearly crushing me to death and severing my spinal cord in half deserves blame for my injuries. But that's his burden to bear, not mine. That life-changing instant is where his guilt lies. What I'm more concerned about now are all the moments after that one. He was in charge of one moment in my life. I'm in charge of all the ones that follow.

When I interacted with my fellow patients at TIRR that gave up, it was obvious that they could not see beyond the excruciating void where life had dropped them. When they made the decision to not push beyond their immediate limitations or, at the very least, try to dig deep enough to find hope, they set themselves back days or weeks. But then there were patients, like my roommate Mitchell, who, instead of reveling in the addictive pain of anger, chose to press on. His fluke accident that changed his life before it had even really gotten a chance to get started wasn't his fault. He didn't choose paralysis, but he did choose how it would affect him.

Observing those around me who threw in the towel was upsetting, but seeing Mitchell and other patients' inexplicable positivity and vigor in the midst of soul-crushing news fueled me. All of us were in the pit together. We had all been thrown into a situation that none of us could have prepared for or wanted, but some of us were joyful and progressing, while others had been swallowed by hopelessness and refused to put forth effort. What was the tipping point between us? I can only guess, of course, but having lived out a tragedy and witnessed others do the same, I whole-heartedly believe that the difference was where we chose to place blame. We all had

89

someone we could blame. Whether it was another driver, a violent criminal or someone across enemy lines, every single one of us had the right to fault someone else with our struggle. But just because we could, didn't mean we should.

For those on my hall at TIRR who essentially gave up, the blame was visible behind the resentment and anger they hung on to. Someone else had caused their pain, someone else had left them in this situation, someone else took away their future with an act of negligence or accident. Their blame was a cage, holding them captive and refusing them the freedom to find their own new normal. On the other hand, I remember lying in a hospital bed that demanded I remember how much had been taken from me while at the same time learning from my roommate Mitchell how good it felt to laugh again. I remember how positive my mom was from the moment she walked into my room in the ICU and throughout my recovery process. Her words were always "You're going to be all right, Tyson. You can do this." The moment I took the heavy weight of blame that I had every right to lay on someone else's shoulders and placed them squarely on mine was the moment my recovery kick started. It wasn't that I blamed myself for the accident. On the contrary, I carry no guilt from that day. I do, however, hold myself accountable for every day since.

If I feel sorry for myself–and I have an hour or two every now and then when that happens–I have no one to blame but me. What happened to me is not my fault, but how I react to it is. The driver of that mixer truck took away my legs, but he will not take away my future. If I blame someone else, I'm essentially handing them over the keys to my life and putting them in charge. I can't change what happened but I can choose to move forward with my life and make it better. It's up to me. And I want to be in the driver's seat.

STEP 3: DON'T SURRENDER.

During my stay at the hospital, the question I–and

everyone else–was thinking was, *Am I going to live?* When I transitioned to TIRR, every day of those first three weeks uncovered something new for me about my condition and I remember constantly thinking and asking, *Is this normal?*

The Turtle Shell was extremely constrictive and, true to its name, slowed down my progress. Wrapping from back to front, my entire midsection was encased in hard medical-grade plastic. That's why after my first three weeks at TIRR they sent me home to recover until the doctors agreed that it would be safe to remove it. Those first three weeks had been difficult, but simple, processes: learn how to get your shoes on, find your new equilibrium in a chair or on a bed, get more informed about your injuries. Until the Turtle Shell was off, the therapists were out of things they could teach me. Once we got the go-ahead to remove it, I returned to TIRR and discovered an entirely different set of expectations. We were past the simple stuff. No more how to roll into a handicap shower or tutorials on how to carry a cafeteria tray on your lap while you roll to your table.

With the Turtle Shell behind me and the second round of rehab ahead, I was ready. I had grasped and come to terms with–at least to a point–that I was in a wheelchair. I didn't like it, but I understood it. My therapists picked up on my energy and declared this round at TIRR as Go Time. The goal? To teach me how to live life from a chair. The days of carefully handling my fragile body fresh from surgery were over. Now therapy sessions meant giving me the know-how to deal with real-life situations and dangers. That meant my therapists often created worst case scenarios for me and then talked me through how to manage the risks. I remember the first day they lowered me down out of my chair onto the ground and coached me through scooting to the other side of the room where I could push up to the edge of a couch and transfer to my wheelchair. It was followed by an exhausting afternoon spent at the bottom of a staircase, where I learned how to lug my body one step at a time to the next floor, dragging my wheelchair with me every inch. Imagine trying to cross a room or climb a flight of stairs using only your arm strength while taking furniture with you. The process was grueling. My dead weight legs were the focus of these exercises, but it was my lack of abdominal muscles that provided the real challenge. With no balance, I fell forward over and over again, losing all progress and having to start from scratch.

By the end of each day, I would pull myself into bed absolutely wiped out. There wasn't a single training session that didn't ask more of me than I felt I could give, but none were more frustrating and tiresome than learning how to independently transfer myself into a vehicle. Most paraplegics choose compact sedans because of the ease with which you can shift from chair to driver's seat. For some reason, a sedan wasn't for me. Instead, we bought a used Toyota 4Runner to replace my totaled Corvette and brought it to rehab. Transferring to an SUV would provide an even greater challenge, but one I had to overcome if I wanted to drive and have the independence I needed.

I rolled out to the parking lot, slide board on my lap, and listened to my therapist give instructions about how I would shift my weight a little at a time until I transferred into the driver's seat. There is little room for error when transferring from a wheelchair into a vehicle, and my mom was such a nervous wreck that she had to go the opposite side of the street to watch. She couldn't bear not to help me. Over and over, I pushed myself up the slide board toward my 4Runner, only to slide back down the inches I had just battled to gain. It took 28 minutes for me to get into the car by myself for the first time. Somewhere around minute 19, I remember thinking, *Forget it! I don't need to drive!* But I knew that wasn't true. Powering through the frustration and the pain of that moment has given me a lifetime of freedom that I would be incapable of having if I had given up in that parking lot.

There have been countless times since then that I've faced the same dilemma. Figuring out how to push a grocery cart and wheel at the same time, retrieving items off of a top shelf without the ability to stand up, and learning how to get in and out of a fishing boat–just to name a few. When the odds seem overwhelming, it can be so easy and convenient to walk away–or, in my case, roll. But if I give up because it's too tough, I'm essentially giving away one of my options. If I had allowed my frustration and anger to win that afternoon in the TIRR parking lot, I wouldn't be able to live as independently as I want. If I had given up, I would have given that part of my life away.

As I look back over the year following my wreck, it was filled with insurmountable challenges and trials that shook me to my core and threatened to steal joy from every part of my life. I'm reminded every day that the choice is still there, but deciding that surrender isn't an option has allowed me to live a life I'm proud of.

KEEP GOING

Life is infinitely more difficult now than it was pre-wreck. Before 2005, when I ran an errand, I would park wherever I wanted, hop out, swing open a door and walk through with little effort. I paid no attention to whether or not there were potholes in the sidewalk or an automatic door for someone with a handicap. Today, when I pull up to a store I'm immediately mapping out my strategy: Where's the handicap spot? How far is it from the ramp? Is there a sidewalk that connects to the entrance?

Before my wreck, if I checked the weather it was to see if I should grab my coat or not before heading out the door. Now a rainy day can collapse my entire schedule. If it's a downpour I've got no options but to be soaked. How am I going to push the rims of my wheels and hold an umbrella at the same time? Even a brief rain shower can fill a parking lot or yard with puddles and soak through your shoes. My shoes are wheels, and those wheels roll through puddles, mud and whatever else debris is on the ground, splashing upward as they spin. Even a short distance through a wet parking lot can leave me soaked and my hands coated in mud from pushing myself forward.

When you add up all of those inconveniences, I have a lot more reasons to be frustrated than I used to. Life is just harder now. I think back to what used to seem inconvenient to me and laugh at myself. I had no idea what inconvenient meant. I do now. I live it. It's why sometimes I feel like I've earned the right to be in a bad mood. That's not an attitude exclusive to the wheelchair crowd. We're all entitled to them every now and then.

The catch? That's all we're entitled to: now and then. Here's the truth I've discovered about bad moods: they can turn into bad days, which turn into bad weeks, which turn into bad months and can eventually change your entire outlook on life. The way we approach problems, and even the good things that happen, has the power to take a single moment and make it linger for years. Today sucked? That stinks. And it's OK to be mad, sad or frustrated. But in a few hours, you have to get going. Because if you loiter in the pit, you might decide to stay there.

That's why I don't have bad days. I might have a bad hour, or two hours, but after that I'm moving on. Some mornings I wake up and it feels overwhelming that my legs don't listen to my brain anymore. If I want to get out of bed, I have to use my hands and lift my legs, one at a time, out from under the covers, then carefully transfer myself into a wheelchair to get across the room. In those first few minutes, full of frustration, my reaction will set the tone for the rest of my day. My goal is not to suppress feelings, but instead deal with them in the moment rather than stuffing them away to fester, only to explode later.

Some people have called me optimistic, and I've been blessed with parents who never doubted me or my abilities, even when the prognosis was devastating. Even so, I don't believe that my positive approach to this new life is a result of only seeing the good and happy side of every day. Instead, I think I'm the opposite. Life chewed me up and spit me out;

this is not what I wanted. But if I'm going to keep moving forward and live a life that I look forward to, I have to take in all the negatives and then choose that the positives are more important.

During the last few days of my rehab, the nurses decided that they could put my hopeful attitude to good use and sent me to the rooms of other patients who weren't dealing as well with the rehabilitation process. I was quickly surpassing the goals the medical staff set for me and exceeding their timelines for my recovery, both emotionally and physically. When I checked in on day one, the doctors had looked me in the eyes and very frankly told me to keep my expectations in check. Rehabilitation, they said, is a marathon, not a sprint. With my level of injuries and setbacks, their experience and education predicted my second stay, after I was released from the Turtle Shell, would last around three months. I completed my therapy and was released after just three weeks.

As we were checking out of TIRR, the same staff who had used me as a motivator for their less hopeful patients, told me about a wheelchair sports camp nearby called Camp Extreme at Camp for All. My therapists were part of the camp staff and had experienced firsthand how beneficial the camp had been for their patients. But instead of inviting me to sign up as a camper, they asked me to serve as a camp counselor.

Having only spent three months in a wheelchair at this point, I was unsure what I could teach others. I still struggled tackling everyday activities and many of the campers would have lived most of their lives in my position. Nonetheless, a month later I was on the campgrounds, playing wheelchair basketball, softball and swimming. I joined in a pick-up game on the basketball court with a handful of guys who had catastrophic injuries like mine that had left them with varying levels of paralysis, and felt a competitive drive surge through my veins again. These were not slow, easy games. We pushed back against defense and blocked shots while shouting harmless trash talk back and forth at each other. I took a turn sitting the bench and watched as my teammates passed the ball back and forth across the court. My ICU prediction had come true. In the face of the worst news I had ever received, I believed then that I could create a new normal that matched the life no tragedy could make me stop wanting. Now here I was, merely weeks later and stronger than even I knew, playing wheelchair basketball just as I had envisioned. I wouldn't experience sports in the same way I always had, but they would still be able to be a part of my life.

Everywhere I looked during that week at camp, people were enduring the same challenges I was living through. It was a week of being shielded from the outside world while surrounded by people who were much further down the same road I found myself traveling. I picked up shortcuts and pointers–like an easier way to get into my chair from the floor–just by observing them and listening to their advice.

On the final day of camp, a couple of the guys invited me to ride handbikes with them through the hill country to nearby Lake Somerville. I was fresh out of rehab and still unsure of my abilities or endurance. I remember asking, "Man, do you think I can?" These guys knew what I was feeling because they had lived it. They remembered the frustration that comes with learning how to live in a body that no longer obeys commands. They knew the uncertainty I was feeling and the weakness that follows extended hospital stays. What's more, I think they knew from experience how an accomplishment like this could change the way I viewed myself and my strength. "Let's try it," they said.

A quick briefing on how to pump the pedals using only my hands and we were off, my body staying securely strapped into place as we sped down hills. My memory may exaggerate, but I'm convinced the route was ten miles each way. We pushed and pedaled with everything we had until we crested a hill, drenched in sweat, then coasted down only to face another one. My biceps and triceps screamed with each turn of the pedals but the thrill of reaching the top of each hill, surrounded by others who understood what it took to get this far, outweighed the pain. We reached the lake and my arms hung down at my side, thrashed. My life wasn't the same anymore, but injury or no injury, wheelchair or walking, it would always be filled with mountaintops and valleys. I would reach the heights of joy and coast downhill easily, only to face a challenging incline that would make me fight my way back to the top. Not being in a wheelchair wouldn't protect me from those ups and downs. But maybe, I thought, looking out over the lake as I rubbed my sore arms, maybe my commitment to press forward against the odds could.

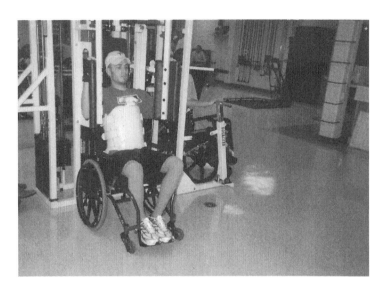

Upper body strength was a vital part of physical therapy since I would now be solely dependent upon it to get me where I needed to go.

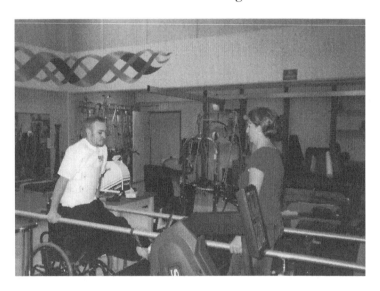

Learning how to shift my weight and relieve pressure on my lower body.

8 "I'M NEW AT THIS."

Before I began living life out of a chair, I had never even heard of a slide board. After my rehab parking lot lesson, it became an extension of my daily life. Every errand, every trip to school, every drive to church was flanked–getting in and getting out of the car–by using the slide board. I wasn't held back, but I was limited. I was only as free as my wheelchair and slide board allowed.

I guess I assumed life would always be that way. I don't think using the slide board was an error in judgment. It made independent living possible in those early months. But somewhere between recovering and recovered, I settled into a comfortable default. I had reached the end of my recovery and was successfully living independently so any further progress, it seemed, was unnecessary and could be halted.

After two years of living independently, I was made acutely aware of how tight my comfort zone had become. This revelation came courtesy of my wheelchair basketball teammates–people with whom I was tough, competitive and capable on the court. The moment I rolled out to the parking lot, however, they watched my demeanor shift to cautious and unsure of myself. It was an eye-opening experience for me to see the confusion on their faces. I can still see how their heads shook back and forth, eyebrows raised, as I placed my slide board carefully between my chair and driver's seat one night after practice. They knew the importance of a slide board–all of us had been dependent upon one at some point in our recoveries–but they also knew I was past that point.

In the early days, using my slide board meant gaining inches, only to lose feet as I slid back down over and over again, away from my goal. The frustration in that learning moment outside of the rehab hospital was so intense that I almost surrendered my keys. But after months, and eventually years of practice, the slide board became part of my routine. It was no longer an essential safeguard. In fact, as my teammates pointed out to me, it had become a crutch without me even realizing it. No one who hadn't lived through my experience blamed me for using one, and I'm not sure someone who wasn't also in a chair could have successfully pointed it out to me. Truthfully, it made everyone around me a little bit more comfortable to see me depending on it, rather than risking a fall. But the guys who shared my paralyzed reality knew what I was doing. I was living two lives–one of fear and one of independence–and my teammates called me on it. I couldn't have known it at the time, but ditching the slide board would become a milestone moment for me, one I would reflect and rely on during tough decisions. I could have kept the slide board; there was nothing wrong with using it. But it wasn't about the slide board.

After my wreck in March, the remainder of the semester was spent in and out of hospitals and therapy sessions, trying to repair my broken body. By summertime, I had big decisions to make. The plan had been for me to recuperate a bit longer, maybe take a semester or two off before returning to the rigors of school and independent living. My body was almost defiant, recovering at a rate much faster than anyone anticipated. "Your body was broken in half," I would hear from those supporting me. "There is no need to rush things." But as I bounced back and acclimated to my new normal, I began to entertain the idea of returning to school in time for the fall semester. If I could swing it, I might even graduate on schedule.

All of my doctors anticipated I would need more time to heal and to relearn how to do life. My back, my life, my plans–everything had been shattered. In their eyes, moving to my parents' home in Midland and taking an extended leave of absence from school was a necessary precaution to keep me from injury, or worse. It had been the plan since my first day at TIRR. But now, having made incredible strides, taking any more time away from working toward my goal felt like moving backwards. There was no doubt in my mind that I had to keep pressing forward. With only two years left before graduation, I could see my goal in front of me. I had worked for years to gain ground–one inch at a time–and sliding backward at this point would have been agony. This would not be my slide board summer. If at all possible, I had to keep moving forward.

THE DEEP END

When my wreck changed everything, I had been living on my own for four years. The idea of leaving that behind to go back home, even to live with family whom I loved and deeply cared for, did not feel like an option for me. I wanted to–had to–keep moving through life.

The finish line at school was now within sight. I hated the thought of throwing four years of college away simply because my legs no longer worked, but unless I wanted to give up on school, or put it off indefinitely, I needed to stay in San Marcos. Quitting was not going to happen, I decided. My mental health was positive and I was learning how to drive so, in my mind, I was good to go. I found an apartment near campus and set out on a path to regain momentum as an independent man. Although it sounds contrary to common sense for someone who needed help to get through each day, living on my own was one of the best things I could have done for my recovery process. I was forced to cook, do laundry, get in and out of a bathtub and clean my apartment without any help. It was Living Life Out of a Chair 101 on fast-forward.

Regaining my independence outside of the TIRR walls brought satisfaction, but also a slight shock to my system. On one hand, I had an almost celebrity status at Texas State University. Everyone on campus had heard my story or quickly caught up once I returned. But it became an uncomfortable guessing game each day as I wheeled across campus, curious as to which friends would be happy to see me, and which would feel so awkward in my presence that they would instead avert their eyes, turn and walk the other way. I don't hold people's reactions against them or assume they meant to be rude. Rest assured, it was uncomfortable for both of us.

My reception was generally warm and my classmates supportive, but there were still painful, stinging reminders that my life was now drastically different. I had to accept my new reality, but it soon came to light that not everyone would volunteer to do the same. When a handful of friends disappeared and became unreachable, it hit home that living out of a chair would set me apart, for better or for worse.

My new mode of transportation changed just about every experience and every interaction I had. A cross-campus commute was now completely different, for one thing. As I rolled to class, I saw everything from a new angle. The hills that I once saw as beautiful were now my adversary. The majority of my classes took place behind the gymnasium in Jowers Center, but a few were in the Quad, straight uphill. Getting there on foot makes for a tough walk, but rolling there would have been a death wish. I soon understood that I would need to find handicap parking not just some of the time, but everywhere I went. I was relearning how to do everything again, and all at once.

To take advantage of closer parking, I needed to get a handicap placard from the university's parking services—an office that was, ironically, at the top of a hill. When I pulled up to the Administration Building, I already had months of experience under my belt assembling and disassembling my chair in parking lots. What I had yet to practice, however, was doing so on an incline. After putting my 4Runner in park, I turned off the ignition and put my chair together, setting it down on the pavement next to me. As I reached back toward the passenger seat to grab my backpack, I remembered one important detail I had overlooked: locking my brakes. I whipped my head back around just in time to watch as my chair rolled downhill, bouncing and picking up speed with every bump.

One of the curious details of my circumstance is that when I'm sitting in a vehicle I don't appear to be disabled. I can't count the number of times people have given me dirty looks, tapped on my hood or even lectured me for parking in a handicap space. I appreciate blending in, but it didn't serve me well that day. A girl walking by on her way to class made eye contact with me and I half-yelled from the driver's seat, "Hey, can you help me?" She took off running. Kudos to her parents for teaching her about stranger danger.

There was absolutely nothing I could do. I was stuck in my car at the top of a hill and my legs were in a ditch at the bottom. I finally convinced a passerby to help and I had to swallow my pride and own up to my situation by saying, "I'm paralyzed and I'm new at this and my wheelchair is at the bottom of this hill." It was a simple sentence but powerful as I look back on it. It was probably the first time I described myself, out loud, with that tagline. I was paralyzed, I was new at this and I would probably have to ask for help a lot more than I wanted to.

THE ELEPHANT IN THE ROOM

Heading back to class at Texas State was at once exhilarating and exhausting. My professors were incredibly understanding and all around awesome when I returned, allowing me to pick up where I left off at spring break. Rather than retake their courses from the beginning, some of my teachers told me to come back to their classes when they got to chapter ten, or wherever they were when I was forced to leave in March. Going to class, like everything else, was different. When you walk into class you can kind of disappear because you're just one in a crowd. When you roll through the door in a wheelchair, there's nothing you can do to prevent sticking out. Things you don't even think about when you can walk were now big obstacles. I no longer sat in a desk. Instead, a table was set up for me on the side of each classroom that I could roll up to. I wasn't set apart on purpose, but it was inevitably isolating. I came on campus in 2003 over six-feet tall and returned three-feet, nine inches. It was a huge hit to my ego.

Because I had always insisted on putting in so many hours at work, I spent most semesters taking the 12-hour minimum course load so I could stay an active student but not cut back on my paycheck. Now, graduating when I wanted to meant cramming in classes whenever I could fit them, including a 2006 summer short course that proved more than I bargained for. Throughout the course's brief three weeks, my class took place upstairs. Normally this would not be an issue, but during this particular summer, the building was being renovated and the elevators were not functioning. On the first day of class I met two guys, classmates, who would be in charge of carrying me in my chair up two flights of stairs to class and back down afterwards. At this point in my recovery, I wasn't always sure what was weird or normal for me at college, but there was no doubt that this one fell into the awkward category. The upside: knowing those two guys would be inconveniencing themselves to wait on me at the bottom of the stairs each morning got me to class on time every single day. No small feat for a night owl like me.

Each moment of vulnerability brought with it a painful transformation that tore away at my pride. I couldn't always do everything on my own, but if I was willing to press forward against these towering obstacles in front of me, a better version of pride, one that came from achievement rather than attitude, would still be waiting on the other side. That hadn't changed simply because I was now in a chair.

The months that followed were filled with learning curves, both in and out of the classroom. My entire life had been filled with sports, running and workouts in the gym. It was what I spent my free time doing and what I was working toward spending a career enjoying. Sports had been my whole life. They were everything to me. If I wasn't playing them, I was studying to coach them. These new factors in my life could prove to be game changers though. Now that the landscape was different, I could sense that I had a decision to make. Either I could still build a teaching and coaching career, or I couldn't, but who was in charge of that choice?

I was filled with doubt, and uncertainty swirled through me even as I went to class to continue the pursuit of a dream that had formed before my life was so severely rerouted. I knew I didn't want to let a wheelchair stop me from doing what I had always wanted to do, but there were other variables to consider as well. What if the kids I coached, my athletes, wouldn't take me seriously? What if school administrators couldn't see my abilities because of my limitations? All of those questions, I decided, came out of a place of fear, not strength. If I couldn't find a school district willing to hire me that was one thing, but if I didn't chase after this goal simply because I couldn't run anymore, then shame on me.

By January 2007, I had reached the final semester of my course load, the point in my degree plan when student teaching would be required in order to graduate. Our professors assigned our matches, placing us with a specific grade level and a teacher who would oversee our progress and give feedback on whether or not we were cut out for life inside the classroom. Even as I got dressed on the morning of my first day as a student teacher, my nerves welled up inside of me. Years of studying could not prepare me for this. I knew how to write a lesson plan and develop curriculum based on state regulations, but the preparation I needed to enter a classroom full of teenagers was not part of any of my course work. Would I spend the whole first week fielding questions about my accident? What if I couldn't command authority in a classroom from a chair?

As I pulled into the handicap space at Hays High School for the first time, my worries began to calm. My overseeing teacher would be Coach Kane, a tough but respected teacher for his results and camaraderie with his teams. I expected student teaching to be mostly observation with a little bit of teaching mixed in for practice. What I discovered instead was that Coach Kane was much more hands-off, preferring to tag-team teach. We would go over chapters together, but he allowed me to design lessons and teach classes on my own.

On Fridays when Coach Kane was out of town for a game, he let me take over his volleyball practices, leaving the students with strict instructions that I was the teacher for the day. His confidence in me brushed off on the students and I never once had a behavioral problem or respect issue. From day one, I felt like I belonged in front of the classroom and on the court. If there is anything in life I'm confident in my knowledge of, it's sports. Every time I had the opportunity to slip into coaching mode, I felt my self-confidence increase and my anxieties subside. Within a few days it became apparent that this path was still the right one. Pressing on toward this goal was exactly what I needed to do.

Dr. Paese, my college professor, would occasionally show up to observe my lectures. His opinion of my abilities would carry heavy weight on my final grade and ultimately my ability to obtain a teacher's certificate. After a few of his random visits, I found out he had nominated me for National Student Teacher of the Year. Even more shocking to me: I almost won.

As my semester of student teaching came to a close, Coach Kane passed out surveys to the students, asking them to give feedback on my performance. The answers were almost entirely positive but a pattern emerged in their responses, revealing one glaring oversight in my method. While I had tried to incorporate my history and the wreck that led to my paralysis and life in a wheelchair into my lectures on physical and emotional health, I hadn't been 100 percent forthright and vulnerable with them. "I wish you would have told us your story sooner" was a common phrase scribbled at the bottom of students' surveys. They weren't trying to be nosy or bully me for details; they simply wanted to know what happened that led me to show up to class every day in this goofy-looking chair.

I had been the teacher, but the students from that semester schooled me on an important life lesson: people just want to know. It's the elephant in every room I roll into. It's not because people are looking down on me or judging my situation; it's just friendly curiosity. Those students showed me that I need to rely more heavily on honesty rather than living life with my guard up. I don't start every conversation with the story of my wreck–that would be weird–but I don't put it off as long as I can anymore. This is my story. To have a genuine friendship or even comfortable conversation with others, it helps if I get it out in the open early on.

It took six years, start to finish, but in May 2007, I finally had my graduation day at Texas State University. As everyone else lined up in alphabetical order and walked down a steep flight of stairs into the gym, I was lowered down to the gym floor on an industrial elevator used to lift carts and stacks of chairs. As my classmates walked in to Pomp and Circumstance, I rolled to my seat on my own. It was another experience where the absence of working legs isolated me and made me stand out, but after two years, I was beginning to make peace with my differences. When my name was called and I rolled up the ramp onto the stage to receive my diploma, shake hands with a school official and take a picture, none of us considered that there would be no place for me to put my diploma while I used my hands to push my wheelchair. Halfway across the platform, the diploma flew off of my lap and onto the stage. I felt the stares of everyone in the arena as I navigated retrieving my diploma and getting back to my spot on the gym floor. There were plenty of moments of awkwardness, for sure. There were fleeting moments of embarrassment, as well. Most of all though I remember feeling incredibly cool. I experienced a life-altering, bone-crushing wreck that I shouldn't have survived and still only missed a few weeks of school. I could no longer stand to write lecture notes on a whiteboard at the front of a class and yet, I was successful at teaching a classroom full of kids and coaching a gym full of athletes. An event that turned my life upside down hadn't prevented me from achieving my goals or from living a life I wanted to live–a life that only months earlier I had been unsure would be worth living. If being run over by a 33-ton cement mixer couldn't hold me back, then, seriously–what could?

With Dr. Wiley, one of my biggest supporters at TSU, on graduation day.

9 PLEASE STAY SEATED

Being saved from death doesn't necessarily mean you're brought back to life. My dedicated team of physicians and physical therapists worked tirelessly and exhausted every option they could think of to heal my broken body. They beat back against death with every resource available to them and against all odds. That I even made it to the operating table with a pulse that Friday afternoon was a major accomplishment. They made it possible for my heart to continue beating and my lungs to draw air, but we all knew those victories were simply the starting gate.

As grateful as I was to wake up at all, waking up to legs that didn't work felt a lot like waking up on another planet. I didn't know how to do life anymore. It's difficult to describe how frustrating it is to be of sound mind and completely aware of how life is supposed to work, but be held captive by injuries. It was tough to wake up every morning and remember that hardly anything was the same. When I rediscovered sports, it breathed life back into me in a way that medicine couldn't. Wheelchair basketball and the occasional spontaneous long-distance arm biking trip scratched that competitive itch, but it was student teaching and coaching that provided the consistency I needed. Sports and I weren't through, and I had to keep pursuing it, even if that meant playing would never again feel or look the way I wanted it to.

It's tough to wake up in a hospital and be unsure about what tomorrow or a year or five years from now will look like. It's far worse to wake up feeling unsure of whether you even want to find out. By getting back in line with the pursuit of the goals and ambitions I had pre-wreck, I was able to reignite my excitement about whatever the future held.

I started going to job fairs, on the hunt for a coaching position anywhere in Texas. My search didn't last long. Before I even graduated, an offer came in from Hays High School, where I had spent a semester completing my student teaching. A job at Hays was a big deal to me. It felt like an even greater achievement than snagging a new job that I had chased down and applied for. The staff at Hays had seen me in action. They knew my work ethic, my teaching style and my abilities, and they wanted me back. What's more, there weren't any openings for new hires at Hays so the assistant superintendent created a position specifically for me. My new role would be as a special education and health inclusion teacher and coach. I was living the dream.

Coaching, of course, was much different than playing. I learned that during student teaching. As a coach, you couldn't just show up. You had to plan practices, get there early and stay late. You had to be the heavy, making sure everyone was staying on task. If someone got out of line, it was up to you to be the disciplinarian and walk the fine line between friendship and authority. It was tough, but exhilarating.

Over the summer, I got word that I would be the coach for the boys' baseball team. I couldn't imagine a better assignment. If there was anything in life I understood, it was baseball. And coaching a team full of teenage boys? It was only a few years prior that I had been one myself. I understood how to create healthy team culture and push them to their limits, but only to make them stronger. I was revved up for the season, and anxious to get started.

But in the world of high school sports, it turns out, rearranging coaching positions is about as common as rearranging furniture. Before the first day of school, word came down that there had been some switches made among the coaching staff. Baseball, as it turns out, wouldn't be my focus. I was still a coach, but for the girls' softball team instead.

I had never played sports with girls. Until this point, my coaching and playing experience had rarely, if ever, been co-ed. I spent the first two decades of my life surrounded by guys in locker rooms, on the field, riding on the team bus, and even at home with two brothers. I knew girls were tough competitors. I knew they had the same drive to win as my fellow male teammates. So I ignorantly assumed that coaching girls would be no different than coaching boys.

I was wrong.

Don't misunderstand me, the girls I coached were incredible athletes. But the level and swings of emotion they brought with them were something I was completely unprepared for. It quickly became obvious that the world of girls' sports, which I assumed was simply a mirror image of the guy version I grew up knowing, was entirely different.

On our first day of softball practice, I described the conditioning exercises we would start with–a model I had used throughout student teaching. I set the girls up running bleachers and explained their stretch and cool down to follow. Before long, I was surrounded. Softball players were puking and crying. They were sprawled everywhere–on the ground by me, leaning against the field's chain link fence and laid out on the bleachers. I felt like I was in the middle of a terrible sports movie, the kind with a fumbling coach who can't even blow the whistle well. Clearly, I was doing it wrong. After that first day, I realized an adjustment needed to be made, but not by the girls. My coaching methods, it turns out, were not one-size-fits-all.

These girls didn't feed off of aggression like the guys I had always been on teams with or coached. The hard-nosed, uptight coach personality that moved male athletes to action was ineffective for my softball players. What they wanted were structured, challenging workouts that helped them improve but kept priority on fundamentals and skills. Of course the girls could work just as hard as their male counterparts, but they needed and deserved to be coached well and in a way that met their specific training needs. The arbitrary conditioning schedule I had always ascribed to wasn't good enough.

I had never worked with female athletes, but it didn't take long for me to decide that I would rather coach a girls' team than a guys' team any day. For starters, my female athletes had an upper hand in competition because of how incredibly coachable they were–far more so than any of the boy athletes I've interacted with over the years. They listened to what I had to say and worked hard to apply it.

During that first year, I was the teacher and coach but my students weren't the only ones who learned. Some days it was my turn. It seems obvious, but coaching out of a chair added a level of difficulty I hadn't considered. I couldn't get up and show them how to follow through on their swing or slide correctly into second base. I couldn't show how to block home plate with your body or the proper stance for the catcher. My coaching style had to switch to include more explanation than demonstration, which grated on me at times. We were both learning. I knew how to do it, but explaining and teaching while sitting down was always challenging. It was a learning curve, but I gave it everything I had.

I launched a softball training program in the offseason, something the school had never offered, and when girls would ask me to warm them up before games, I didn't hesitate to roll out in front of the crowd to play catch on the field. Most games I would sit on the first or third baseline and help direct runs. My teams made playoffs both years and even had the opportunity to compete on the intimidating and immaculate Texas A&M softball field. The girls who I coached as freshmen went on to win the state championship as seniors, a feat they earned solidly on their own, but one I take pride in having had a small part in making happen.

Throughout those two seasons of softball coaching, I never had a single problem with any of my teams. Maybe they took it easy on me because I was in a chair, but I have a feeling that, had they not respected me, they wouldn't have held back on sarcasm or insults. I refused to be the coach who sat in the dugout or on the sidelines simply because I was stuck in a chair. Not just because of my pride–although I would have gone crazy without being fully involved in every game and practice–but because my athletes deserved better than that. They didn't care if I was in a chair or not. They depended on me and I needed to show up.

It was a little bit of a shock to my system when I found out I'd been switched from a sport I knew better than anything else to an entirely new challenge. I was pumped to coach baseball, but, I'll admit, wasn't sure how much I would enjoy coaching softball. But their skill, hard work and commitment (and lots of wins) showed me how much I could enjoy the unexpected. I was "Coach D," as they called me, and I loved it. If I went back to full-time coaching today, softball would undoubtedly be on the top of my list. I enjoyed every minute.

A couple of times a season, I'll stop by to watch the Little League games of one of my close friend's kids. I'll sit in my chair in the heat, baseball cap pulled down low and watch as he and his teammates step up to the plate and run after pop flies. I'll cheer them on and try to will my muscles to remember what it felt like to run and swing a bat. I don't harbor any bitterness. Those moments aren't even bittersweet in memory for me. But man, was baseball fun. It's pretty easy to miss.

There are days when it's tough to stay seated. Maybe if I had naturally been shorter before my injury, it wouldn't be so difficult to swallow now. I used to walk into a room and be a head taller than most of the people around me. I could see what was on top of the refrigerator and was the guy you asked to help you get that box off of a high shelf. Now I look up to just about everyone. Often, it's simple things that I miss. Sometimes I just want to jump up and hit the top of a door frame or get something out of the top of the freezer, for goodness' sake. But usually when those melancholy moments hit me, it's somehow related to sports.

It doesn't take much to make those memories kick in. Football fields and baseball diamonds have their own distinct smell of dust and freshly cut grass mixed with sweat and adrenaline. I know, it sounds absolutely disgusting, but for me, it's home. For a moment, even now, I can close my eyes and transport myself to the outfield—my hand clenched in a glove, stadium lights reflecting off fan-filled bleacher seats—every time I roll onto the playing field as a spectator or coach. My memories don't care that I can no longer stand at home plate. In my mind's eye, I'll always be on the team.

LOUD AND CLEAR

Coaching put me back on the field when I wasn't sure how to move forward. I credit sports and coaching with a hefty part of my positive outlook and mental recovery, but I was left with a nagging question: Without sports, who am I? I would imagine it's a question that every athlete has to ask themselves after they get cut from the team, an injury sidelines them or they age out. Once my ability to walk was taken away by the wreck, that question held even more weight. I had already been forced to figure out who I was without legs. It was a terrifying but satisfying experience to discover I was still me. Sports were a big reason I came out OK on the other side of that crisis, but without it, my life was a question mark.

I had dedicated so much of my focus to working toward being a coach before life turned me upside down and literally tore me apart. I would now never again play sports the way I always had. What if circumstances changed again and suddenly coaching wasn't an option either? What if I chose to move on to something else? Would I still be able to tap into that same fire and drive that kicked in whenever sports were concerned, even if I was no longer a part of the team?

It was a fear that I'm not sure I could acknowledge, even as I was starting my career coaching. It wasn't until later that I recognized it as a concern that had been bubbling unnoticed just beneath the surface. It's funny, though, how life gradually weaves new themes and talents and passions into your personality, piece by piece, thread by thread, until all at once you realize the pattern you expected to see in your life has been replaced with something much bigger and much better than you knew possible. That's how I felt about teaching. I knew teaching would be an important part of my profession, but it was never the goal. Coaching was the party; teaching was simply the vehicle that got me there. And yet, during my two years at Hays, I began to see how my teaching made an impact, maybe even more so than my coaching.

Teaching doesn't typically come with a lot of pats on the back or atta-boys. It's the daily commitment to make a difference in the life of a kid, whose positive outcome you probably won't be around to witness. But whether they knew it or not, my students gave me an incredible compliment when, over and over, I would hear, "Coach D, we forgot you were in a wheelchair." We would be getting ready to review films in practice or getting resources from the library and a student would ask me to hand them a remote or a book that was sitting on a ledge well outside of my now 3' 9" reach. I'd smirk and say, "Come on, seriously?" and they'd laugh as they remembered I couldn't stand up. It wasn't the wheelchair I was glad they forgot. It was the barrier. If they didn't connect with my teaching style or with me personally, they wouldn't have had any trouble remembering.

When I began my teaching career, my goal was to match. I was positive that my wreck and my story didn't need to be hidden, but I also didn't believe that it needed to be brought front and center either. My capabilities as a teacher wouldn't be diminished by my disability, and I wanted to prove and illustrate that to the kids I taught and coached. I had the potential to make a difference, I knew, and I didn't want my wheelchair to stand in the way of that opportunity. I didn't necessarily want to fit in, I just didn't want to be so different that my voice couldn't be heard. Student teaching revealed to me that my handicap, my life in a chair and the story of my wreck instead made every word that came out of my mouth louder and more powerful. My wheelchair didn't silence me, it handed me a megaphone.

THE TEACHER BECOMES THE STUDENT

It's always surprising to look back and see how giant life changes happen in the tiniest of moments. My baseball career all but ended with one lousy warmup throw that tore up my shoulder. My wreck happened along an unassuming back road on a cloudless Friday afternoon. And it was over chips and salsa at a Chili's in Buda, Texas, that a new chapter of my life began.

Dr. David Wiley had invited me to dinner to catch up one evening over summer break. I had just wrapped up my second year of full-time teaching and coaching, and he was curious to hear about my experience. Dr. Wiley had been one of my toughest health professors at Texas State, but he was also one of my biggest advocates. After my wreck, it was because of his leadership and backing that the university allowed me to pick up where I left off at school, without having to repay for classes or start from scratch.

Between bites, he leaned over the table and casually asked me, "If you weren't teaching and coaching, what would you be doing?" It was the same question, worded a little differently, that had been a lurking concern of mine for years: "Who am I without sports?" It was a defining moment for me. Somehow, hearing it from someone else made more sense, and without hesitation I knew the answer. "I'd love to be a motivational speaker." I heard the words come out of my mouth before I even realized they were true.

From that one sentence emerged a new direction for my life. Ever my supporter, Dr. Wiley put me in touch with two of his colleagues, Kevin Tutt and Michael Daggs, who had a small agency that represented public speakers. It was unbelievably cool to entertain the idea of becoming a professional public speaker, but I had no idea where to start. When I made the call to Dr. Wiley's contacts they (understandably) blew me off for about a month. I had no experience. I had no training as a speaker. I wasn't giving up, but I also understood their doubt. I got a courtesy call from them about a month later, politely explaining that they weren't hiring at that time. I didn't argue, but instead told my story, and their answer changed to "Wait, we might have something here."

That was it. I made a complete career switch, quitting my coaching job in order to pursue a life lived out on stage. Before the summer was over, I was holding a mic and telling my story to a group of students. My words were awkward and my nerves worn thin in those early presentations, but I knew I was on the right path.

I spent my life chasing a dream. Being a coach and teacher was the only career I ever imagined myself doing. When I switched into a speaking role, I didn't surrender that goal. In my view, it is the exact opposite. I loved helping kids grow. I loved instilling new workout regimens that allowed them to be better athletes. I got energized by explaining new concepts to students and seeing their light bulb moments when it all made sense. And I got a thrill out of inspiring my co-teachers and empowering them to push past their own obstacles simply by sharing my story. With public speaking, I get to do all of that, just on a much larger scale. I get to speak at training camps and student council conferences and teaching seminars. I'm still teaching. I'm still coaching. My classroom just got bigger.

One of the great things about being a teacher is that by default you can't help but also be a student. If I don't keep growing and changing and improving, my lessons and pep talks and speeches will become stale. I'm lucky because my wreck has made me a lifelong learner. Every day is a new challenge and carries with it something new to overcome. It's made me nimbler. I have to be willing to change and adapt because I can't just step over obstacles or take the route everyone else is following. I had to figure out how to wash dishes without being able to stand over the sink, how to drive without being able to press the pedals and live independently without someone else leading the way. And the list goes on. Some days it can be a pain, but for the most part, my inconveniences are a gift.

My life is not even on the spectrum of what I imagined it would look like when I was a child, teenager or college kid. And that's OK. I've found that sometimes the best parts of life come out of the most unexpected and–yes–even painful events in our past. If I hadn't already had a mindset of accepting change as a necessary part of life–courtesy of my wreck–I wouldn't have been able to take hold of this new career and make it my own. My dream was a good one. But being willing to step out into the unknown made it even better. I didn't stop dreaming because of my wreck. I just learned to dream bigger.

Telling my story from the stage.

Switching to a bigger classroom.

10 WHAT'S YOUR WHEELCHAIR?

I didn't choose life in a wheelchair. It chose me. I didn't drive down Five Mile Dam Road that Friday afternoon in March thinking a wreck was waiting for me just a little further down the blacktop. I didn't wake up in the ICU, groggy from anesthesia and expect to be paralyzed from the waist down. And I didn't begin my recovery expecting it to end with me being pushed out in a wheelchair. I didn't choose change. It chose me.

And odds are, you've been chosen, too. Our stories are different. Your legs are likely still able to carry you wherever you need to go, but even so, you've probably got your own wheelchair. Your wheelchair isn't getting you from Point A to Point B like mine. Yours is different, but it threatens to do the same thing that any regular wheelchair will do if you allow it to: hold you back. Yours comes in the form of distractions like work conflict, relocation, family upheaval, illness and anxiety. Our stories are different and the details probably don't match up, but in some ways, the ups and downs of all of our storylines are the same: no matter how hard we work or how focused we stay, there will always be unexpected curves or bumps in the road that we'll have to somehow learn to navigate.

While our stories are similar, my change brought with it different consequences. When I roll into a room, it's easy to see what my change was because it's not something I can hide. If you get laid off or go through a tough break up, it will most certainly affect your life. There will be emotional or monetary effects and your friends and family will notice and feel the aftershocks of your pain for a while, but that's as far as it goes. You can go to a restaurant or the movies or a car wash, and no one can tell by looking that you're experiencing a job transition or that your girlfriend decided to call it quits. You'll still feel the pain and it will certainly still affect you, but there are refuges available where no one knows the details. For small pockets of each day, you can retreat and hide if the pain of change gets too intense. Refuges like that don't exist for me. There are no places full of strangers where I can go that won't immediately be met by eyes that can see the effects of change in my life. And that's one of the reasons I choose to talk about my challenges from the stage. Because if you have small glitches at work or minor conflict at home, those hurdles can be easy to run away from. You can sweep them under the rug and pretend they didn't happen. I can't escape my obstacles. They're here to stay.

It's another one of those blessings I wouldn't have asked for, but am thankful to have. If my challenges had been easier to hide, I probably would have. I don't have that luxury, and because of it, I truly believe my life is better for it.

Unexpected disruptions are a part of life. You could ask anyone off the street about their life and it probably wouldn't take long for them to come up with a handful of painful obstacles they are facing. They're easy to come by. If you've somehow escaped them up until this point, I can assure you that the road won't always be quite as smooth in the future. That's not me being cynical; it's just a fact of life. I hope the challenges on the horizon will be small and easy for you to overcome, but even if they're not, how you respond will determine how you come out on the other side of them. When those problems come up, you'll have a couple of options:

1. You can pretend they aren't happening and refuse to deal with them.
2. You can withdraw and nurture resentment and anger.
3. You can face change head on.

The year following my wreck was a textbook case study on how disaster can make or break a person's spirit. I had a front row seat, not only to my own dramatic and horrific tragedy, but to the earth-shattering changes in the lives of others as well. During my extended stays in the ICU and TIRR rehabilitation hospital, I watched as my fellow patients and rehab roommates each chose a different option. The results of their choices were both predictable and consistent.

For those who chose to live a life of pretend, refusing to acknowledge their crisis, I can tell you with absolute certainty that it was impossible for them to move forward. It didn't matter how many visits the therapists made to their room, or how attentive and affectionate the adorable therapy dogs were that had been sent to cheer them up. No one could give them instruction or advice that could break through the wall of ice they had built between themselves and reality. They were frozen, stranded between what they wanted to be real and the unexpected changes that now made every second feel, look and seem different.

When my rehabilitation process sped up, and the nurses decided to capitalize on my positive outlook and commitment toward recovery by sending me to visit patients on my hall who weren't responding well, I got to interact on a personal level with people who were living lives of denial. I rolled into each room, certain of my choice, but unsure of how to sell the same focused determination to someone who wasn't buying in. I remember how surprised I was at just how visible misery was on their faces. They didn't want a pep talk because they didn't need what I or any of the educated and experienced medical professionals had to say. They were somehow exempt. If they put off acceptance long enough, begging everyone to act as though their personal catastrophe never really happened, they could prolong the feeling that it never did. They could extend the timeline, making the life they lived pre-change comprise more of their story. If they could fend off this life shift for a little longer, maybe, even though the most irrational patient knew it was impossible, they could will their wish to be true.

Throughout my weeks at TIRR, I had multiple roommates, each with a unique approach to their injuries. Our shared time in rehab was usually short, as sometimes they would graduate out of therapy and go home, or they'd be moved to a different part of the unit to focus on a specific part of their recovery. Each time the bed was switched out and a new face was pushed into the room on a rolling hospital bed, I was reminded how even though our injuries might be identical, our recoveries would not always be the same.

My first roommate's chart could have been a mirror image of mine–we both endured a complete break at the T-12 vertebrae–but the difference between us was stark. Our timelines were completely different, for one thing. My injury had occurred only weeks prior while his was a few years old. Our spinal injury, it seemed, was the only thing we shared in common.

I began noticing differences the moment he was wheeled into place a few feet away from me on the opposite side of the room. For starters, his bed didn't look like mine. A contraption I had never seen before had been built as an attachment that stretched parallel to his body the length of his bed. A-frames were at the head and foot, and a long metal pole stretched between them. I silently tried to imagine what it could be used for, mulling options over in my thoughts. Did it support his weight? Did they use it to stretch his leg muscles? I was dumbfounded, but I only had a month of rehab experience under my belt. Maybe that same bulky equipment was in my future, too.

Everything made sense the following morning when his family had stepped away for a moment. The pole, it turns out, was his backup plan. Even though he had been injured years ago, his recovery quickly went stagnant. He had gone home to live with his parents, understandably, but from there, it seemed, he made no further progress. He had essentially given up. It was the mood given off by everyone in the room, with him leading the way. When he wanted to roll over, he said, he would call for his parents to come and physically do it for him. If he couldn't wake them up or get their attention, he would grab onto the pole and use it to shift his body, a few inches at a time, until he could move into the position he preferred.

I was shocked. Here was a man whose profile matched mine in so many ways. Our injuries aligned almost perfectly. We both had supportive families willing to encourage and care for us, and we both had access to excellent medical care. And yet, in three weeks' time, I had already surpassed the benchmark he settled for a long time ago. He had invested years of his life in rehabilitation. On the outside, it appeared he was trying but anyone who spent more than a few minutes with him could see through that exterior. His denial had set the tone for the entire family. He wasn't willing to push past his limitations, which meant the responsibility and brunt of the burden fell to his family to help him function on a very basic level.

The most heartbreaking to watch, however, had to be those who withdrew themselves from their everyday life. They were desperately hurt. We all were. Every single one of us who ended up physically mangled in the ICU or the spinal injury floor at TIRR had throbbing heartache. It was excruciating, both physically and emotionally. It meant that relationships with everyone from parents to girlfriends to lifelong friends required more work and extra care. For those who refused to engage, to reside and wallow in their pit instead of looking for a way out, their pain only multiplied.

Anger entered my room early one morning during the middle of my second stay at TIRR in the form of a new roommate. In his late fifties, he was a surly war veteran whose leg was claimed by an IED during battle. We shared a space for a few days, and during that time, he did not receive a single visitor. No family, no friends to check on him. It's hard to know where his bitterness began. Whether it was his experience in wartime and his amputation, or the lack of support that shaped his attitude wasn't clear. Neither was it clear whether his bitterness was what drove those around him away, or if their absence simply intensified his suffering. What was clear was his dogged determination to make everyone he encountered endure at least some of the anger he lived with every day. He wasn't violent. I don't remember him ever throwing anything or even yelling at the staff, but it was apparent in every demand barked through tight lips at those working diligently to help him that the assistance he so desperately needed was the very thing he was unwilling to accept.

I want to clarify that every one of us struggling to push beyond our injuries and limitations experienced an element of resentment during our recovery. Regardless of our personalities or family support, the process just ignited anger. It was infuriating that we had to learn how to do basic stuff that only weeks prior we were doing without permission or instruction. I was a 22-year-old man who had to relearn how to take a shower on my own. It was OK to be mad.

Anger just came naturally as we went through these humiliating processes with our family and friends as an audience. But temporary resentment wasn't a problem. Savoring that pain and clinging to that anger, however, was. I watched people around me as their bitterness created a lifestyle to which others weren't invited. Even when family and friends found a way to edge their way past the walls their loved one had carefully constructed, it was frequently too painful to stay there. A life of anger is almost impossible to live without spilling it out onto everyone else around you. When emotional injury is that intense, the only way to survive is to siphon some of it off onto others to carry for you. But no one should have to bear that weight forever.

It would be too simplistic to say that everyone I met during my recovery process could be pigeonholed into only one of three categories. Truth be told, most of us found ourselves in all three at one point or another. I say with complete honesty that while I stumbled, I have spent most of my life post-wreck looking change in the eyes, head-on. But for one reason or another, too many were unable to hold that gaze. They wavered back and forth, alternately pushing loved ones away until the isolation became too great, and then gathering them back into their lives under the condition that everyone agree to go along with their denial.

They deceived themselves into believing that anger gave them power when instead it acted as an anchor. They remained stuck, relentlessly weighed down so that they were never given an opportunity to rise to the top for air or hope. I think a lot of my co-patients expected their denial and isolation to protect their loved ones. They believed that by keeping others at arm's length they could contain the pain. But, from my front row seat, it only seemed to create even more.

OWN IT

My story isn't perfect, but no one's is. Most stories are difficult and messy, filled with embarrassing blooper reels and things we'd rather forget instead of regret. Our stories are strange combinations of change and consistency, conflict and joy all wrapped up in one. My life-altering tragedy intensified all of those experiences, handing me some changes I wasn't ready for, but affecting my life and character in ways that I sincerely appreciate. Mercifully, tragedy isn't the only way to get those same results.

These imperfect stories of ours are real, with real

consequences and real pain along the way. Some of us will survive better than others, but your outcome and how those speed bumps affect you doesn't have to be left to chance. I know, without a doubt, that change can break someone's spirit, but I'm living proof that it doesn't have to. If you're willing, it can take you to another level of self-awareness, gratitude and empowerment instead.

We've all seen someone needlessly crash and burn. We've watched from the sidelines and held our breath, then face palmed and shook our heads when they dropped the ball. Their potential and their future and the next level was right there in front of them, but something got in their way. They got cut from the team, lost a family member, or didn't get the scholarship they hoped for, and suddenly, they called it all a loss. Plan A didn't work out, and I agree, that sucked. But it's called Plan A because there's also Plan B waiting in the wings. And guess what? Behind that is Plan C, Plan D, Plan E, and so on.

Living life out of a chair wasn't my Plan A, either. It was more like Plan Z or Plan No Thank You. But this giant adjustment in my life has brought so many gifts along with it that I couldn't have anticipated. I don't mean that in a cheesy "I'm so grateful because I realize how much I could have lost" kind of way. I have tangible benefits as a result of that hot Friday afternoon and the wreck I found myself a part of. I've met and influenced more students, teachers, athletes and administrators through my public speaking career than I ever could have in the classroom or on the field. My vision for my future was clear before my wreck, but I could never have even dreamed how it could be supersized, magnified and multiplied into what it is today. I've discovered what I'm capable of, and it's better than I could have even known to dream before this gigantic, plan-altering change in my life.

I've seen over and over again how a startling change can initially cause upset, and then an even better result. If that's going to describe you, as I hope it describes me, an unwavering determination is a great starting line. From there, putting your finger on what part of the change frustrates you is next. Is it the change itself, or the side effects that are the most difficult part for you?

It's the meet-and-greets after my talks on stage where the most meaningful conversations usually occur. It's where kids will open up about friendship dramas, or executives will let their guard down to discuss the painful after-effects of moving their family across country for a job promotion. Those are the situations when I emphasize to people that diagnosing the root of their hurt and anger is vital because it can radically affect how they approach the issue.

A rift with a close friend or a move to a new state with new hobbies and new people isn't going to ruin your life, nor does it mean the potential for good things is behind you. It means that specific fragments of your life–your social life or friendships or family–will need extra TLC for a while. It may create areas that will require more investment and hard work, but you're up for that challenge. Don't pretend that the family friction or struggle with your own identity after a crisis is something you can't affect simply because an unwanted change was handed to you. You get to decide how change will affect you. It's not up for grabs and out of your hands. Your loved ones are depending on you to take ownership of your choices. Stop pretending it didn't happen, let go of the anger that wants to destroy you and face that change head on.

TAKE CONTROL

There's a dirty little secret about this change stuff though. If you haven't experienced change, you may think you're just extra lucky or put together. Sometimes when big changes are affecting everyone else but not us, we think we're either doing something wrong, or worse, we assume we're just better, or trying harder than everyone else. And maybe that's the case for some people. The catch is, however, if you're not experiencing change, it might be time to make one.

Change is a scary word that can strike fear into most of us.

We like our comfort zones and our giant orange safety cones around our neat and tidy plans. My story is so terrifyingly full of change that wherever your comfort zone is, I'm about 100 yards to the left. And that's why I roll out on stage, through the butterflies and nerves that don't go away even after more than a decade in front of audiences, because I'm here to share the good news that I've been to the edges of our comfort zones and back and I can tell you that while, yes, it's sometimes scary, it's worth every ounce of courage it takes to get there.

If you've been avoiding change you need to hear this difficult truth: you are the only one who can steer your future. When you're in middle school and high school, it's easy to think that it's the parents and guidance counselors and teachers and coaches who clear the path for you to reach your dreams. When you're an employee, it's tempting to assume that your boss is responsible for how far you climb and how big your achievements can be. And I can tell you from personal experience that when you're a teacher, it's natural to feel limited by school resources, expectations and pressures from state regulators. But those assumptions are just distractions. Dumping the responsibility of your future—your life—on someone else's desk only slows you down.

What change do you know you need to make and what's holding you back from making it? Do you need to extract yourself from some bad influences? Would a lesser-paying job that's more in line with your career goals be a better fit? Is there some family or friendship conflict that you need to gracefully confront?

Everyone has to deal with change eventually. Students and board members and CEOs experience unique and different obstacles, but in the end, their response to those curve balls will affect them all in similar ways. And you, too, have been or will be surprised by tough new obstacles that threaten to hold you back. You'll discover your own version of a wheelchair in your life that you'll have the option to surrender to or overcome.

When change rears its head and stares you down, it's a signal that big, important choices need to be made. When your knees are shaky and your palms are sweating and you aren't sure which path to choose, take a deep breath and try to picture yourself a day, a week, a year down the road. Will avoiding necessary change benefit you in the days to come or will it set you back? Will pretending that your family's big move across the country never happened make it easier to make new friends, or will it leave you sitting alone at lunch? Will the frustrations of a conflict at work cause your anger to boil underneath the surface until it negatively affects your career, or should you own up to your part and face it with courage?

When you look beyond the immediate discomfort and pain to the possibilities of the future, it makes it easier to make the right choice. As you encounter the obstacles in your path or realize that change has chosen you, too, you'll be able to identify which direction will bring the most benefit. Once the right path becomes clear, tie your shoes and get walking. What are you waiting for? None of those wheelchairs could hold you back.

Wheelchairs only hold you back if you let them.

11 INSIDE OUT

I've had a lot of people ask me over the years about the what ifs in my story–those small details that could have changed my wreck's outcome and its ramifications forever. Even though they can sometimes be uncomfortable to answer, I can always sense the well-meaning intentions behind those questions. My history, with its twists and turns and near-misses with death and love and disaster, can feel a little more movie-like than reality. From my seat, it's just life, but I get that for others, hearing my story feels like a suspenseful watching experience where you leave the movie theater and spend the drive home replaying the details you wish had been different.

The moments after my speaking gigs, when I get to interact with the audience one-on-one, is always my favorite part of any event. It's when I hear what part of my story makes a difference and when I learn how to better reach and inspire others. It's also when the what ifs linger behind polite small talk, waiting until they apprehensively break through the chatter. Audience members will ask:

What if you had been driving a bigger car?

What if you had turned left sooner?

What if you had stopped for gas and ended up at the scene

just a bit later instead?

Those are tough questions for people, and I know asking them takes bravery. They're loaded questions for me, though, because while I sense the caring nature that they stem from, I never know what answer will comfort the person asking. I agree, it is unsettling to think that had I stopped to top off my tank or grab a Dr Pepper at the 7-11, I might not be in a chair for the rest of my life. But no amount of that second guessing and alternate endings can change my current situation.

More often, people will ask those questions but take an optimistic angle. I always appreciate the effort and attention they take to couch their curiosity in the positive rather than the negative. From their perspective, had the intricate details of that day and the order of their events not aligned as perfectly as they did, I would not be alive today. They'll ask:

What if the volunteer firemen hadn't been on location at the elementary school just a moment away instead of 15 or 20 minutes away?

What if Ryan and Daryl and Phillip hadn't been willing to put themselves in harm's way?

What if the STAR Flight helicopter hadn't arrived so quickly?

So many things had to happen for me to survive the wreck and those what ifs, framed so optimistically, highlight their importance. I was saved by quick-thinking volunteer firemen who saw my wreck from a distance and immediately called in specialized trauma teams. I'm alive because three real-life heroes braved the flames and wreckage to untangle my mangled body from the remains of my sports car. I'm alive because I was on the operating table at the hands of skilled surgeons in a matter of minutes, rather than hours. I'm alive because of people who did more than they had to and cared about someone they didn't know. I'm alive because they listened to their own what ifs. They asked themselves:

What if I don't help?

What if I just watch from the safety of the side of the road until the professionals get here?

What if I just keep driving?

They asked themselves those questions and instead of allowing themselves the easy way out, which no one would have questioned, they stepped up and took the important and messy steps of getting involved.

A word of caution here: what ifs appear to be simple questions, but they're not nearly as harmless as they seem. They are influential catalysts that I've seen deploy in my own life at the most pivotal moments. What ifs can propel you forward and into action, as they did for Ryan and Daryl and Phillip, or they can anchor you below your potential. The key is wielding their power correctly by asking them at the right time and with the right motives.

I remember feeling full of self-doubt and my future full of uncertainty when I was considering going back to Texas State University after my wreck. It was those worry-filled questions, in fact, that nearly kept me from finishing. I was asking myself:

What if I can't remember what I've learned so far?

What if everyone stares at me?

What if my friends walk away from me?

As you know, I didn't let those concerns hold me back. I finished on schedule and rolled across the stage filled with pride. But I want to be absolutely honest with you: some of those what ifs came true. I did have to backtrack sometimes to catch up in classes. I spent some time in tutoring and extra study time outside of class working with my professors to get back to where I needed to be. A lot of people did stare at me. It was a new reality for me that was true on campus then and is true today. Whether I was pushing the rims of my wheels to enter a classroom or intentionally falling out of my truck and into my chair in the grocery store parking lot, I have always been and will likely always be greeted with curious eyes and lingering stares. And yes, unfortunately a lot of my friends didn't stick around after my legs quit working. There were plenty of uncomfortable moments and lots of hard work, but my world didn't come crashing in as the what ifs wanted me to believe it would.

I don't mean to trivialize the pain that lurked behind the hesitations and worries of that time in my life. It wasn't my favorite thing that some of my biggest fears materialized. Some of them inflicted a lot of heartache that I carried with me for a long time–like when some of my closest friends chose to start screening my calls and heading the other direction as soon as they saw me. But as I pressed beyond my doubts toward the finish line of my goals, I was pleasantly surprised that the anxiety I felt around those fears coming true didn't last long. The sting was sharp, but I was too busy moving forward to dwell on its pain.

NO ONE HAS A BETTER VIEW THAN YOU

When my wreck happened, I wasn't a wheelchair guy. A wheelchair guy, in my opinion, is someone born with a disability who has never known what it is like to walk. For years, I viewed myself instead as a guy who got placed in a chair. I wasn't one of "those guys," and I didn't want to identify myself any other way. I remember my reluctance in the early months, when someone else in a wheelchair would see me and recognize my amateur level at this wheelchair thing, and try to give me pointers or a pep talk about how I could still accomplish great things. I wasn't ready to hear it yet. Being in a wheelchair was something that happened to me–it wasn't me.

Over time, I have realized that while sometimes labels are hurtful and being unfairly branded can leave you feeling pigeonholed or insulted, my label was, well, correct. I was a wheelchair guy. I am a wheelchair guy. Just because I can remember what it's like to stand up and stretch my legs or quickly maneuver from room to room and task to task doesn't take away from the fact that this is now my truth.

I was willing to work hard on my physical rehabilitation from the moment I started recovery, but the mind game that accompanies trauma of that magnitude is a whole other story. When you so easily fit into a category, as I do as a person who lives life out of a chair, it can be difficult to take hold of your own narrative. I think everyone deals with that same issue on some level. For some people, it's being deemed bossy or unqualified, too shy or too opinionated, simply because of their personality. When I played college ball I was categorized as a "jock," and all my life I've been described as a "country boy" because of my thick Texas accent and love for all things fishing and hunting. The labels may be different–chatty, weird, loser, quiet, brownnoser–but the feeling they leave behind is pretty predictable.

There are negative descriptions behind each of those labels, for sure. When the only way someone knows to describe you is by your label, it can be demeaning because everyone is more than a one-word moniker. I am a country boy, of course. I grew up in Andrews, not a big city. But depending on how that label is used, I can either be proud to wear it or feel criticized by the person saying it.

The same goes for my "wheelchair guy" brand. I will always be described as someone who lives life out of a chair. The only way that becomes negative is if I allow it to be so. If I take hold of my history and control my story, "wheelchair guy" means only what I want it to mean. As I've matured and grown, that label now stands for courage, accomplishment and more emotional and physical muscle than most people walking around on two working legs could muster. Being a "wheelchair guy" doesn't mean I'm incapable. It means I've climbed bigger mountains than most people would ever dare.

If I didn't own my very obvious label, the alternative would be allowing everyone else's view and opinion of me to define who I want to be and the limits of my potential and ability. That is both unacceptable and unrealistic for me.

I've seen this played out in classrooms, on the field and even in corporate settings. When I speak to people and learn more about their backgrounds and level of contentment and joy in their current situations, I can almost always see who has a hold on their own story and who does not.

In my experience, people who feel on the outskirts or unaccepted by their peers typically do one of two things: isolate or incorporate.

For some people, they hear the labels and go into hiding. Let me be clear here, I don't view that as cowardly. I can relate and empathize with that coping mechanism. Even today when the labels and the stares from strangers start to close in on me, I'll notice myself incubating in my lake house, turning down invites from friends and skipping church to sit alone on my dock. Some days I just don't want to deal with the stares, questions and awkward moments. But after a while that seclusion, which began as a healthy reset button, begins to affect my mood. I can see how all that time alone has sent me into a spiral of over-analyzing and overthinking, of focusing on the negative rather than the positive. And suddenly, out of nowhere, my optimistic outlook has been traded for the sinking feeling that I'm stuck.

Pity parties like that don't start out so pitiful. They begin as a way to escape when we feel threatened, as a way to boost our spirits when many of the voices around us want to tear us down. But I can tell you firsthand that they always leave us worse off than they found us. Long-term isolation is the same animal with a different name. Separating ourselves in order to escape our labels unfortunately has a way of reinforcing them—not to others, but to ourselves.

It's not always easy to pull myself out of that alone time so I usually start slow. Any time I sense the self-loathing or wallowing coming on, I typically start by hitting the drive-thru. If it's lunch time, I'll grab a meal. If not, I'll order something small, but I always follow it up by paying for the order of the person in line behind me. When I'm drowning in the labels and find myself pushing others away as a means to protect myself, I have found that helping others, even in a safe, small way, can always bring me back to the surface for air.

From there, calling up friends to hang out, going to

Sunday morning worship or planning a weekend fishing trip with my brothers helps me shake off the funk that settles in after a self-inflicted quarantine. Hitting the gym usually helps me kick start my motivation. The key is remembering that everyone is responsible for their own course. If I'm going to change mine, it's up to me.

Observing the friendship patterns of the kids I've taught or spoken with over the years, I've seen how finding even one or two peers who share a common interest can provide them with opportunity to incorporate and create a new circle of support. Looking for people subjected to similar labels or forms of isolation can be a great place to start, because they get it.

It's unfairly applied labels that can make you feel like who you are and who you can be is already predetermined–that everyone else, from the outside looking in, has a better view. Whether you see yourself as a slow learner or socially awkward, whether you're held back by a lack of financial means or legs that won't work, no one gets to decide your limitations. No one, that is, except you.

FIVE MORE MINUTES

What ifs are not without purpose. They are what we ask ourselves as a way to prepare and protect ourselves in the face of something that scares us. When we recognize that they also have the authority in our lives to both give and take away power and options, we can see them for what they are– warning lights alerting us to change, not alarm bells signaling us to turn and run.

For me, the what ifs represented my post-wreck social fears: Would I fit in? Would I be excluded by my friends? Would I lag behind my classmates?

I knew I wanted to return to Texas State, to grab that diploma knowing that I had earned it, and to not give up on my career goals. But what ifs are forceful and very rarely quiet. I couldn't ignore those concerns. My only option, I decided, was to do exactly what I have now seen many do so eloquently after my presentations: I flipped my negative what ifs into positives.

Instead of *What if I can't remember what I've learned so far?* I asked, *What if I don't continue learning?*

Instead of *What if everyone stares at me?* I asked, *What if I hide away and no one notices me?*

Instead of *What if my friends walk away from me?* I asked, *What if this will reveal relationships that are truly authentic?*

By harnessing the scary what if and transforming it into a positive question, it became a mental negotiating tool to turn to in the face of absolute uncertainty. Panic had no place to land when my mind was steered toward what I could gain rather than what I could lose. When our heads and hearts are stalled out in fear, the Inside Out What If? removes blinding roadblocks so we can more clearly see the road ahead of us.

Asking those questions the right way can set you on the right track, but they're also a multipurpose tool to keep you accelerating in the right direction.

By asking ourselves what would happen if we gave a little more, helped a little more, connected a little more, worked a little more, we can better envision where our potential can take us. The simplest way to start that process is by asking what would happen if we spent five more minutes each day doing what we know would get us closer to our goals.

Maybe that's five more minutes talking to our loved ones, five more minutes studying, five more minutes working out, five more minutes listening. Five minutes is barely a commercial break but it can make a big impact in the long run. Once the results start rolling in, it's almost impossible to not want to spend even more time focusing on making those goals happen. When it becomes a habit, five minutes can easily morph into ten minutes, fifteen minutes and so on.

My senior year of high school, my baseball coach, Coach Halsey, understood the effect of committing a few additional minutes and giving more than was asked. He was one of those coaches who cared about his players beyond the stadium. He saw sports as more than a game. To him, our efforts on the practice field and during game time were preparing us for the challenges life would inevitably throw us as we graduated and grew from boys into men. His pep talks after practice included an extra five, or maybe ten, minutes every day that helped us see how these practices and drills were getting us ready for something bigger. One afternoon, sweat dripping off our noses in an after-practice huddle, he passed small slips of paper around the circle. The words on those pages, he told us, were his commission to us. He reminded us that none of us would win all the time, that we would have losses come our way and some of them would be big, but he wanted us to stay focused and consider the bigger picture for our purpose. The paper read:

THE GAME OF LIFE PRAYER

Dear God,

Help me be a good sport in the game of life. I don't ask for an easy place in the lineup. Put me anywhere you need me. I only ask that I can give you 100 percent of everything I have. If all the hard drives seem to come my way, I thank you for the compliment. Help me to remember that you never send a player more trouble than they can handle with your help.

And help me, Lord to accept the bad breaks as part of the game. May I always play on the square no matter what others do. Help me study the book so I'll know the rules.

Finally, God, if the natural turn of events goes against me and I am benched for sickness or old age, help me accept that as a part of the game, too. Keep me from whimpering that I was framed or that I got a raw deal. And when I finish the final inning, I ask for no laurels. All I want is to believe in my heart, I played as well as I could and that I didn't let you down.

Amen.[1]

It only took him a few extra minutes that day to print off that prayer and pass it around to his players. He didn't go to great lengths with an elaborate presentation or awards ceremony. It was low-key and quick, but meaningful.

Something about that prayer clicked with me. I wasn't sure what detail was the most powerful, but I remember thinking it was important enough that I needed to remember it. I folded the quarter sheet of paper over a few times, pressing the creases until it fit into a corner of my wallet. I carried it with me throughout high school and into college, never re-reading it because the words were etched into my memory. Every time I opened my wallet, just the glimpse of the paper would flash its powerful meaning across my thoughts and reset my attitude while I chased my goals.

On the day of my wreck, everything that had been in my Corvette was annihilated by the fiery explosion that happened only moments after Ryan, Daryl and Phillip extracted me from the debris. As I lay recovering in the ICU, the responsibility fell to my parents to visit the junkyard and see what, if anything, could be recovered from my car's remains. My dad searched every charred crevice, seeking something that could be brought back and provide a sense of normalcy for me in the midst of absolute chaos.

My Corvette, which was only a few years old at the time, salvaged for a meager $200. There was nothing left that hadn't been destroyed. Even the scraps consisted of burnt upholstery, twisted wires and warped metal. As my dad dug through the remains, he discovered that the console, in between the driver and passenger seats, was still somewhat intact—enough so that my wallet was still inside, waiting for me where I left it when I climbed into the driver's seat a few days before in the university parking lot. He reached in and pulled it out, singed and blackened so that it fell apart in his hands as he opened it. My money, my credit cards, my driver's license—everything was incinerated, melted and unusable. As he carefully laid open its burned compartments, the creased, worn sheet of paper, given to me by a high school coach as an afternoon practice afterthought, slipped out and fell into my dad's hands, miraculously untouched by flames. This old, simple prayer printed off on a dated copier survived when everything else was devoured. A five-minute investment by a high school coach now spoke directly into the most difficult blow I had ever received.

When I was cognizant enough to understand, my dad handed me the tattered paper and for the first time in a long time, I re-read its words. New lines jumped out at me, now as fresh as the pain of my injuries.

"If all the hard drives seem to come my way, I thank you for the compliment...Help me, Lord to accept the bad breaks as part of the game...Finally, God, if the natural turn of events goes against me and I am benched for sickness or old age, help me accept that as a part of the game, too."

Tears formed hot in the corners of my eyes. I knew those words but they rang true now more than ever. The worst what ifs in that prayer had come true. Those memorized lines were no longer poetry, they were actions to live out. The hard drives had come my way, as they do to all of us, whether they take out our legs or break our hearts. In the toughest games of our lives, when the wind gets knocked out of our chests, it's not the bad breaks–the unchangeable pain–that determines whether it's a win or loss. It's how well we dust ourselves off and get back in the game.

1. *The Game of Life Prayer*, paraphrased from Richard Cardinal Cushing's "The Game Guy's Prayer" from Record Group I.08, Series IX–Prayers, Box #64, Richard James Cushing Papers, 1921-1970. Reprinted with permission from the Archdiocese of Boston.

With Ryan Turner, whose brave choice saved my life,
12 years later at a speaking event.

With my STAR Flight cavalry at the 10 year anniversary of my wreck: Kevin, J.R., my parents and Stef.

12 SCARRED FOR LIFE

I don't like using the word "helpless" because I'm not. I am fiercely independent.

I have my own bass boat and chose a house on the lake so I can throw a line in the water whenever I want to, which is most days. The same goes for hunting. I have a rugged track chair, with big, army tank-style tracks on either side that let me crisscross through the Texas Hill Country, past thorny mesquite trees and thick underbrush, until I find the perfect vantage point or reach the deer blind. But independent as I may be, guiding that boat into the water and detaching it from the boat trailer, and maneuvering from my everyday chair into my hunting one requires another set of hands–or, honestly, legs–to safely do so. Wheelchair life just naturally creates more moments of vulnerability than I'd like.

Living life to the fullest while dealing with limitations can sometimes leave you in situations that aren't ideal. They're the types of stories you don't tell your mom, for fear they would leave her sick to her stomach with worry. It was one isolating evening in Kingsland, Texas, surrounded by miles of empty woods and the sound of nothing but birds overhead and the thumping of my heart pounding in my chest, that proved to be one of those times.

My buddy Travis and I had spent the morning bird hunting until the heat took over and we packed it in for lunch. We were heading back out for another round just before dusk when my track chair started acting up. The sand and crushed granite in the low water crossing of the Llano River were bogging down the chair's mechanisms, leading it to let out a sluggish whine from time to time. This distressing sound might have been a sign that someone less stubborn would have heeded as a warning. I, of course, decided to keep heading toward our planned hunting location, refusing to stop for something as minor as a wheelchair malfunction. We reached our lookout without any problems and it turned out to be the perfect spot. Before the sun even began setting, we met our legal limit and had to call it a day.

As we headed back to the truck, the track chair's whine grew more and more drawn out, morphing from a quick squeal to a long, low grumbling moan. Every press of the joystick, signaling it to move forward, was met with increasingly delayed responses. It decelerated until it finally lurched, and then stopped dead. I tried pressing against the joystick again. Nothing. I checked the connections that were visible from my seat to see if we were lucky enough to have a quick fix on our hands, like a loose wire or a rock lodged in the crevice near the joystick. No such luck. I looked at my friend Travis who was standing a few feet away in stunned silence. We stayed that way for a few moments, realizing the situation we were in.

It was still daylight and miserably hot, but the truck would still be a good 20-minute walk away through some tough terrain for Travis. It had been no problem for my track chair on the way out, but getting it back would be a different story.

To be clear, there is no pushing a track chair. It is a different breed of wheelchair, with tracks shaped more like triangles than circles for wheels, and comprised of gears wrapped with an extra sturdy conveyor belt. If the gears don't move, the tracks don't, either. No power means no movement, and my track chair was completely powerless.

Travis got behind me and pressed his shoulder into the back of the chair, digging in his heels and pushing as hard as he could. I budged only inches. The sun would set soon and figuring our way out of this mess would get infinitely more difficult. We weighed our options. Travis offered to throw me over his shoulder and get me back to the truck, but that was a terrible idea for lots of reasons. My pride being one.

It was 100 degrees and sweat dripped off of us even as we remained still. Travis repeated the grueling pushing process—in flip flops through sand—until he had nothing left. We sat in the blistering heat, Travis in his ridiculous choice of footwear for a hunting trip, and me wearing hunting boots that would never touch the ground, bouncing ideas back and forth until we settled on a game plan that involved splitting us up. At that point, Travis called a friend, a local game warden, and enlisted him to gain permission for Travis to cut across neighboring private property and bring his vehicle through the only truck entrance available.

I watched him leave and felt the quiet sink in. I was literally stuck. I had witnessed my friend pour himself out to rescue me until he crumbled in a heap on the burning sand. It was a terrible feeling to be fully dependent on someone else's hard work. My chest puffed outward as I swallowed the pain of being bound physically and against my will. I didn't just want to participate, I needed to participate. I needed to not be helpless. I took a deep breath, placed my hands into the grooves of the gear-driven belt and shoved. I pitched forward, making painfully slow progress, but progress nonetheless. Again and again, I pushed on the grooves, moving a few inches at a time in the direction that Travis had taken off. Sand and crushed granite caked onto the belt and my hands scraped with every push, as though grinding against hot sandpaper. Half an hour passed. My biceps and forearms began to tremble with exhaustion, the sun simultaneously burning the back of my neck and face as it beat down and then reflected off the pale ground. I leaned my head back to catch my breath as the familiar sound of a diesel engine sputtered through the brush, and Travis pulled into the clearing near me. Blood now covered the multiple tears that had formed in my palms and my hands fell open in my lap as I braced myself on the armrests and twisted backward to see how far I had come. Two hundred yards of embedded chair tracks stretched behind me, every one a symbol of my determination. I couldn't save myself, but I could do my part, even when no one expected it of me.

Sometimes, when the actions of other people or life's surprising and unexpected trials are outside of my control–like my experience that day in Kingsland–it can heighten the sense that my restrictions are bigger than my abilities. I didn't choose this difficult life. I can't choose how others will react to my limitations. But I can choose how I respond.

There are some daily concerns for me that will never go away. They're not the pretty, perky motivational tools people like for me to speak about from the stage. They're the gritty, painful, dangerous side of this life alteration.

There's the run-of-the-mill daily aches and pains that result from sitting still all day–the back pain from being unable to properly stretch, the shoulder soreness from relying too heavily on my upper body for movement. Then there's the pain that can escalate from a tolerable annoyance to an excruciating disruption, like my legs, which are in a never-ending, constant state of pins and needles. It's the same feeling you get when your foot goes to sleep in the car or your hand goes numb when you doze off on your arm. It is a distracting feeling that demands your attention until you can successfully shake and knead the blood supply back to where it belongs. Except, for me, the tingling never stops.

That daily ache in my legs and butt can ignite into a full-blown burning sensation after I've sat in one position for too long. As someone who never stands up, that means it happens every day, sometimes multiple times a day. Road trips are the worst instigators, which is ironic since my career as a public speaker means I'm driving across the state or country most of the time. When I pull up to the hotel or conference center, I'm usually desperate to shift my body. The burning is similar to an itch that demands to be scratched or trying to hold back a coughing fit. By the time I collapse out of the truck into my wheelchair, wheels locked on the pavement, my nervous system is under the impression that I've suffered second-degree burns.

Then there's the dangers that no one else even thinks about in a world made for walking. Cracked, sunken pavement can jar me out of my chair if I'm not focused, and cars parked illegally in the only wheelchair-accessible spots can mean long treks across a parking lot through weaving cars who can barely see me over their steering wheels. But most of the dangers are ones only I notice.

For most people, a simple scratch means a Band-Aid. For me, it can mean isolation or even death. I was grabbing lunch one afternoon at a Tex-Mex restaurant during my last semester in San Marcos when a patch of gravel caught my wheel and threw me out of my chair, landing me directly onto my backside on the asphalt parking lot. I was shaken, but thankfully my injuries were negligible, leaving me with only a minor wound on my butt. The location of the injury, however, meant it would receive constant friction from my chair and would require special attention.

Ordinarily, I would stay out of my chair for a week or two and let it heal, but at the time, I was student teaching and absences weren't allowed. I had come so far. I was so close to completing this long, drawn-out journey to my diploma and teaching certificate that I could see the finish line. Bowing out now (because of a scratch!) was more than I could accept. I trudged forward, noticing that with each week, the scratch was not only not healing, it was getting worse. By the time I rolled across the stage to grab my diploma, I needed professional wound care.

I had been warned about pressure sores in rehab. In a life skills class at TIRR they passed around gruesome pictures while explaining how they were wounds that developed from the inside out. My scratch, which previously would have scabbed over and healed, was now unable to do so. I knew they were dangerous and could lead to infection and all of that, but the magnitude of what I was dealing with did not hit me until my first trip to Baylor Wound Care in Fort Worth.

Imagine getting a cut on your elbow. It's not a terrible one. Maybe it bleeds a little, then clots and quickly scabs over. Now imagine that your cut elbow is in constant contact with a surface–an arm rest, a table, a chair–never getting a break, not even for a moment. Every instance of contact reopens the wound, preventing the healing process. Eventually, that wound which has remained fresh will slowly worsen every time it is reinjured. That's how it was with my parking lot crash. My wound was never given the opportunity to repair itself. Every moment of my day was spent with all my weight resting on it in a wheelchair. Every time I shifted my weight or pressed against the chair's rims and surged forward, my body leaned and the seat or my jeans would brush against the wound. Each reopening was almost imperceptible, but the collective result was devastating. My situation was only made worse by a lack of fat and muscle tone in my atrophied lower body. By the time I graduated, my bone was visible through a wound the size of a quarter. I had a pressure sore.

The doctor snapped me back to the reality of my situation with his prescription for almost total bed rest. I was allowed to get out of bed to eat, shower, use the restroom and leave for one outing each week. Otherwise, I had to be in bed and was absolutely not allowed to be in my chair. The medical staff scraped the sore to encourage new skin to grow–which was as comfortable as it sounds–and ordered me to bed for two months. The alternative would have been surgery and skin grafts with no guaranteed success. There was the possibility that infection could set in if I didn't take this seriously. Death was not out of the realm of possibility.

I was a good patient, albeit a stir-crazy one, and I spent a good part of May, June and July under the covers with cabin fever. By mid-summer, my pressure sore had healed itself. As I rolled out of the wound care center after my last appointment, all of the staff ran out to greet me by the reception desk, rang a bell, threw confetti and yelled, "This is Tyson's last day because he beat the pressure sore!" That's how big of a deal it was. Confetti and celebrating were involved.

From the moment I wake up, until the moment I fall asleep, the possibility of pressure sores is on my mind. I'm constantly shifting my weight, watching for hazards on the ground and protecting myself from things that are dangerous only to me–like the hard concrete entrance to a swimming pool when I lower myself into the water or long drives without pit stops to stretch.

There are things I can't do anymore–like not worry about dying from a scratch, for one. There are relationships that have changed or been lost because of the way my life has shifted. But probably one of the most frustrating things that has changed has been my inability to rely on my own skills or handiwork, rather than hiring someone else to fix or make or assemble something. I hire a landscaping company to keep up with my small yard that would, pre-wreck, have taken me less than an hour to knock out. I find myself having to call up a friend to help me install a new battery on my truck or make a simple engine adjustment–not because I don't have the necessary skills, but because I can't leverage the weight properly from my lower angle or reach the bolts with my limited range. It's exasperating to have to call in help to accomplish something I know how to do on my own, but can't.

It was a point of conflict for me as a man that I could live independently but still be reliant on others in so many ways. I remained optimistic, but those tasks which required me to call in backup were setbacks for my confidence. I had imagined in rehab that if I was truly going to continue life on my terms and the pursuit of my goals, I would return to life as I had known it before, just minus the legs. That's not been the case.

Processing that change was one of the most difficult parts of my recovery, until a frank rebuttal from one of my friends.

TYSON DEVER authored with SARAH PAULK

We were sitting in the lobby of a conference center, waiting for my turn on stage, when he said, "You know, you used to be able to do 100 things, and now you can do 90. It doesn't make the 90 any less important just because you can't do the other ten."

He threw those two sentences out so casually that it caught me off guard when his words crashed into me, realigning my point of view. From where he stood, I was no less effective, no less independent, no less valuable, and had no less potential, simply because of my injuries. Yes, there are things I can no longer do on my own or at all, but that doesn't determine or limit the impact and importance of what I can do.

Even with my defiantly positive outlook, I had unknowingly been focusing heavily on what I no longer was, on the gaping holes left behind in my life. I was weighed down by the negatives, the awkward phone calls to ask for help and the stares that come with the territory. I was limiting myself without even realizing it.

That simple exchange shifted my perception. From that moment on, I decided to focus on what I can do. Why would I assume that my remaining 90 would have less worth now that I had lost ten? Nothing about that 90 had changed. I would always notice the aching absence in my life initiated by the permanent loss of the use of my legs. But that permanent change did not invalidate the rest of my life. Why would I focus on the things I can't do, when I can focus on the things I can?

MY (NOT SO) SECRET FORMULA

Before my wreck I never really noticed how fragile every day is. Each one is filled with multiple choice options about everything from whether or not to hit the snooze button to what to eat for lunch. Most of them are trivial, but the fragility comes into play over time, as those insignificant choices add up.

154

This is the truth that procrastinators (gulp, like me) hate to hear. We don't like being reminded about how our tendency to put things off for a few more days or months or years can snowball. By definition, we get great joy in absolutely deceiving ourselves that we'll be better equipped, better prepared and more excited about the task later. It's never now and always later.

If we're honest, we know that non-procrastinators are right when they love to (frequently) remind us that the secret to success is wrapped up in one simple decision: Choose to deal with the tough stuff now.

It would be difficult to narrow down in one sentence what that tough stuff was for me. Rehab, recovering from surgery, learning how to do the basics all over again–my post-wreck list goes on and on. Losing the ability to move my legs was, obviously, number one on that list. My attitude was cheery about my condition, but it would be dishonest to say I didn't cling to hope that I would somehow regain the ability to walk.

The day I accepted that I would never again be a person who could walk was when I finally started to really live life again. There are people in situations similar to mine who every day, all day, are obsessed with wishing and wanting to walk again. I am not one of them. I think this is one of the most common misconceptions surrounding the wheelchair and paralyzed communities. If I gathered ten of my wheelchair buddies together right now and asked how many of them really want to walk, I don't think any of them would raise their hand. Don't get me wrong. We would all love to walk given the right circumstances. If someone could provide us the opportunity to walk like we used to–without nerve pain or risk of losing the limited range of motion and abilities that remain–it would be an incredible gift. But we're not willing to endure the options that are currently available to us, like robotic suits that make us feel like the Terminator or wheelchairs with hydraulic lifts that enable us to stand but are too cumbersome to be practical. There are some who believe people like me need to walk or need to at least have the ambition to walk at all costs in order to reach contentment. To me, that says more about the other person and how inadequate he or she views my current situation as a wheelchair-bound person than it does about me. I'm enough. I don't need to walk or spend my life consumed by chasing options that could make me walk again for me to be happy. I'm already happy.

This is not the same as giving up. Instead, it's about choosing contentment while residing in the middle of circumstances that cannot be changed. Facing the unchangeable tough stuff head-on won't get easier with time. It's not something that procrastination can soothe. For me, it was like ripping off a Band-Aid. No amount of effort, optimism or research was going to restore my leg function. I wanted more options, but once I realized none were available, I had to come up with the next game plan. I chose three important actions that represented moving forward for me, and then committed to them wholeheartedly:

1. Set goals.
2. Invest in the lives of others by putting them first.
3. Do my part.

Continuing or starting that three-step process in the midst of painful, permanent change helped land me and keep me on the right track. It's the same formula I follow when I'm relentlessly reminded that I stick out or am viewed by others solely as the "wheelchair guy." Goals keep me focused on the future. They remind me that I still have skin in the game and that I need to keep improving, learning and growing. That's especially important when people expect less of you and want to treat you a little more delicately because of your limitations. Switching the spotlight from yourself to others, even if that just means buying their lunch, wards off the selfish tendencies that tend to blossom in that environment.

On days when it would be easier to fall back on the support of others, I reflect on the road behind me: from the sound of a freight train running over me to the darkness that followed, from waking up in a world full of unknowns to rolling out with the certainty that some things in my life would never change. I have come so far and demonstrated to myself and to those around me that these challenges and obstacles will not be able to prevent me from living life on my terms, chasing down goals and participating in the things that bring me joy.

Knowing that about myself makes all the difference when a new complication appears. Overcoming new challenges sometimes means remembering that I've done it before. I'll reflect on that day in Kingsland. I'll remember my bloody, torn hands and the ground I gained–inches that turned into impressive progress–against odds that said I couldn't. I'll think back to how I survived surgeries and rehab and a wreck that did its best to take my life. I'll remember that I have what it takes. I know because I have the scars to prove it.

When the road ahead seems overwhelming, and your confidence in your ability is waning, take a moment to remember how far you've come. Think about the struggles that at one time threatened to overpower you, but are now just dust in the rearview mirror. Remember the hard battles– sickness, financial strain, a tough job or an incredible loss– that led you to grit your teeth and fight back until you crossed the finish line as the winner.

Life will throw you some incredible curveballs. Some of those pitches will turn into home runs, while others may send you back to the bench defeated. Life will build distracting speed bumps, or even giant lane blocks along the way, but those obstacles are not the end of the road for you. Take inventory of your past victories, learn from previous stumbles and claw your way to the finish line, crawling the last few inches if necessary. You have what it takes. And odds are, you've got the scars to prove it.

ABOUT THE AUTHORS

Tyson Dever is a professional public speaker who specializes in speaking to student groups, schools and corporate teams. His multi-year partnership with Teens in the Driver's Seat, a division of the Texas A&M Transportation Institute, and funded by a grant from the Texas Department of Transportation, has given him an even bigger stage, placing him in front of thousands of students each year to illustrate the dangers of distracted driving. Tyson resides on Lake Lyndon B. Johnson outside of Austin, Texas, where he lives independently, hunts with the use of a rugged track chair and loves to fish from his bass boat.

Sarah Paulk is a professional writer, editor and collaborative author. After graduating from Abilene Christian University in 2004, with a degree in Integrated Marketing Communication from the department of Journalism and Mass Communication, she became a regular contributor to nationally distributed magazines, and has been featured in supplements to *The Wall Street Journal* and *USA Today*. She has ghostwritten for a *New York Times* bestselling author and was a contributing author to the book *The YouEconomy: Join the Movement that Is Changing the Way We Work and Live*. Sarah lives in Fort Worth, Texas, with her husband, Brock, and their two children.

LEARN MORE & CONNECT WITH THE AUTHORS

Want to learn more about Tyson Dever or invite him to speak at your school or corporate event? Visit www.tysondever.com for more information and to see real-life footage from the aftermath of his wreck and the days that followed.

Want to continue the conversation?
We'd love to connect with you online.

Tyson Dever
@tysondever
www.tysondever.com
www.facebook.com/TysonDeverSpeaker

Sarah Paulk
@saw99a
www.sarahpaulk.com
www.facebook.com/SarahPaulkAuthor

90146905R00102

Made in the USA
Columbia, SC
27 February 2018